THE

ARMS
RACE

Opposing Viewpoints

# THE ARMS RACE

## Opposing Viewpoints

by
David L. Bender

OPPOSING VIEWPOINTS SERIES

Greenhaven Press
577 Shoreview Park Road
St. Paul, Minnesota 55112

No part of this book may be reproduced or used in any form or by any means, electrical, mechanical or otherwise, including, but not limited to photocopy, recording or any information storage and retrieval system, without prior written permission from the publisher.

# "Congress shall make no law... abridging the freedom of speech, or of the press."

first amendment to the U.S. Constitution

The basic foundation of our democracy is the first amendment guarantee of freedom of expression. The *Opposing Viewpoints Series* is dedicated to the concept of this basic freedom and the idea that it is more important to practice it than to enshrine it.

# Contents

# Why Consider Opposing Viewpoints?

---

*"It is better to debate a question without settling it than to settle a question without debating it."*

Joseph Joubert (1754-1824)

---

### The Importance of Examining Opposing Viewpoints

The purpose of this book, and the Opposing Viewpoints Series as a whole, is to confront you with alternative points of view on complex and sensitive issues.

Probably the best way to inform yourself is to analyze the positions of those who are regarded as experts and well studied on the issues. It is important to consider every variety of opinion in an attempt to determine the truth. Opinions from the mainstream of society should be examined. Also important are opinions that are considered radical, reactionary, minority or stigmatized by some other uncomplimentary label. An important lesson of history is the fact that many unpopular and even despised opinions eventually gained widespread acceptance. The opinions of Socrates, Jesus and Galileo are good examples of this.

You will approach this book with opinions of your own on the issues debated within it. To have a good grasp of your own viewpoint you must understand the arguments of those with whom you disagree. It is said that those who do not completely understand their adversary's point of view do not fully understand their own.

Perhaps the most persuasive case for considering opposing viewpoints has been presented by John Stuart Mill in his work *On Liberty*. Consider the following statements of his when studying controversial issues:

9

If all mankind minus one were of one opinion, and only one person were of the contrary opinion, mankind would be no more justified in silencing that one person than he, if he had the power, would be justified in silencing mankind...

We can never be sure that the opinion we are endeavoring to stifle is a false opinion...

All silencing of discussion is an assumption of infallibility...

Ages are no more infallible than individuals; every age having held many opinions which subsequent ages have deemed not only false but absurd; and it is as certain that many opinions now general will be rejected by future ages...

The only way in which a human being can make some approach to knowing the whole of a subject, is by hearing what can be said about it by persons of every variety of opinion, and studying all modes in which it can be looked at by every character of mind. No wise man ever acquired his wisdom in any mode but this.

## Pitfalls To Avoid

A pitfall to avoid in considering alternative points of view is that of regarding your own point of view as being merely common sense and the most rational stance, and the point of view of others as being only opinion and naturally wrong. It may be that the opinion of others is correct and that yours is in error.

Another pitfall to avoid is that of closing your mind to the opinions of those whose views differ from yours. The best way to approach a dialogue is to make your primary purpose that of understanding the mind and arguments of the other person and not that of enlightening him or her with your solutions. One learns more by listening than by speaking.

It is my hope that after reading this book you will have a deeper understanding of the issues debated and will appreciate the complexity of even seemingly simple issues when good and honest people disagree. This awareness is particularly important in a democratic society such as ours, where people enter into public debate to determine the common good. People with whom you disagree should not be regarded as enemies, but rather as friends who suggest a different path to a common goal.

## Analyzing Sources of Information

The Opposing Viewpoints Series uses diverse sources; magazines, journals, books, newspapers, statements and position papers from a wide range of individuals and organizations. These sources help in the development of a mindset that is open to the consideration of a variety of opinions.

The format of the Opposing Viewpoints Series should help you answer the following questions.

1. Are you aware that three of the most popular weekly news magazines, *Time*, *Newsweek*, and *U.S. News and World Report* are not totally objective accounts of the news?
2. Do you know there is no such thing as a completely objective author, book, newspaper or magazine?
3. Do you think that because a magazine or newspaper article is unsigned it is always a statement of facts rather than opinions?
4. How can you determine the point of view of newspapers and magazines?
5. When you read do you question an author's frame of reference (political persuasion, training, and life experience)?

Many people finish their formal education unable to cope with these basic questions. They have little chance to understand the social forces and issues surrounding them. Some fall easy victims to demagogues preaching solutions to problems by scapegoating minorities with conspiratorial and paranoid explanations of complex social issues.

I do not want to imply that anything is wrong with authors and publications that have a political slant or bias. All authors have a frame of reference. Readers should understand this. You should also understand that almost all writers have a point of view. An important skill in reading is to be able to locate and identify a point of view. This series gives you practice in both.

## Developing Basic Reading and Thinking Skills

A number of basic skills for critical thinking are practiced in the discussion activities that appear throughout the books in the series. Some of the skills are:

*Evaluating Sources of Information* The ability to choose from among alternative sources the most reliable and accurate source in relation to a given subject.

*Distinguishing Between Primary and Secondary Sources* The ability to understand the important distinction between sources which are primary (original or eyewitness accounts) and those which are secondary (historically removed from, and based on, primary sources).

*Separating Fact from Opinion* The ability to make the basic distinction between factual statements (those which can be demonstrated or verified empirically) and statements of opinion (those which are beliefs or attitudes that cannot be proved).

*Distinguishing Between Bias and Reason* The ability to differentiate between statements of prejudice (unfavorable, preconceived judgments based on feelings instead of reason) and statements of reason (conclusions that can be clearly and logically explained or justified).

*Identifying Stereotypes* The ability to identify oversimlified, exaggerated descriptions (favorable or unfavorable) about people and insulting statements about racial, religious or national groups, based upon misinformation or lack of information.

*Recognizing Ethnocentrism* The ability to recognize attitudes or opinions that express the view that one's own race, culture, or group is inherently superior, or those attitudes that judge another race, culture, or group in terms of one's own.

It is important to consider opposing viewpoints. It is equally important to be able to critically analyze those viewpoints. The activities in this book will give you practice in mastering these thinking skills. Although the activities are helpful to the solitary reader, they are most useful when the reader can benefit from the interaction of group discussion.

Using this book, and others in the series, will help you develop basic reading and thinking skills. These skills should improve your ability to better understand what you read. You should be better able to separate fact from opinion, substance from rhetoric. You should become a better consumer of information in our media-centered culture.

## A Values Orientation

Throughout the Opposing Viewpoints Series you are presented conflicting values. A good example is *American Foreign Policy*. The first chapter debates whether foreign policy should be based on the same kind of moral principles that individuals use in guiding their personal actions, or instead be based primarily on doing what best advances national interests, regardless of moral implications.

The series does not advocate a particular set of values. Quite the contrary! The very nature of the series leaves it to you, the reader, to formulate the values orientation that you find most suitable. My purpose, as editor of the series, is to see that this is made possible by offering a wide range of viewpoints which are fairly presented.

David L. Bender
Opposing Viewpoints Series Editor

# Introduction

*"Human rights, civil rights, women's rights are
meaningless before the greatest issue of all —
nuclear war and our survival."*

Brigadier General B.K. Gorwitz, U.S. Army

Albert Einstein was once asked how a third world war would
be fought. After a thoughtful pause, Einstein replied that he
was not certain of the answer to that question. But the war after
it, he responded, "will be fought with stones."

It might, perhaps, be an exaggeration to state that a worldwide nuclear war would result in humanity's regression to a
new stone age. Conversely, only a terminal optimist would
believe that humankind could shortly restore whatever
progress it was enjoying prior to a nuclear holocaust. The cost
of a nuclear war would extend far beyond the immediate
casualties and disruption of essential products and services.
As the Japanese cities of Hiroshima and Nagasaki have taught
us, the long-term genetic and psychological effects of nuclear
war would be incalculable to both survivors and their
descendents alike. However, Dr. Einstein's prediction does
underscore the fact that the arms race, especially as it relates
to the development and stockpiling of nuclear weapons and
delivery systems, is the most significant issue facing the
contemporary world. Before it, all other issues are, indeed,
"meaningless."

Relevant statistics best illustrate the extent and insidious
nature of the nuclear arms race. Translated into terms of
destructive capability, they present an ominous picture.
Combined, the U.S. and U.S.S.R. today possess strategic
nuclear weapons with the killing force of 16 billion tons of TNT
or roughly 4 tons of TNT for every living human being. These
figures include neither the hundreds of smaller, tactical
nuclear weapons* deployed by both superpowers nor the
stockpiles of other nuclear powers. And significantly, they do

---

*The bomb which leveled the city of Hiroshima in August 1945 had the
explosive power of 20,000 tons of TNT. Today, a bomb of that size is
considered tactical.

not reflect such planned space age exotica as anti-ballistic missile lasers, space stations and satellites, the development and deployment of which will accelerate the alleged need for more sizable and/or less vulnerable nuclear delivery systems.

Many questions have arisen related to the issue of why worldwide nuclear armaments have been permitted to reach such an advanced stage of "overkill." This anthology of opposing viewpoints endeavors to deal with four such questions: Why Is There an Arms Race?, Do Nuclear Weapons Provide Security?, Are Nuclear Weapons Immoral? and How Can the Arms Race Be Stopped? These topics were selected since they are, in the opinion of the editor, the subjects most frequently discussed today in popular, scientific and scholarly forums on nuclear armament and disarmament. Beginning with statements by the U.S. Department of Defense and the U.S.S.R. Ministry of Defense, the viewpoints attempt to provide the reader a broad and integrated spectrum of ideas on the nuclear arms race. They represent the opinions of a wide range of knowledgeable persons and policy making bodies, many of whom are directly involved in decisions governing the possible production and reduction of nuclear armaments.

The editor believes that this anthology will serve as an introduction to the military, diplomatic, economic, political and moral ramifications of the nuclear arms race. However, he also believes that the more informed reader will find much of value in the arguments contained herein since many of them are derived from sources not readily available in public and school libraries. Moreover, an appendix of organizations (one of four appendixes) has been compiled and most of the organizations are directly involved with the issue of world armaments. The purpose and scope of each group is outlined and a mailing address is provided. It is recommended that these organizations be contacted as they are invaluable avenues for further research.

Questions related to the arms race are among the most sensitive and pressing facing the community of nations today. Accepting this and recognizing the limitations of editorial judgement, the editor has attempted to achieve a fair and balanced representation of ideas, thereby leaving the reader to decide where the answers may lie. If the reader completes this anthology sensing the complexities and perils inherent in the nuclear arms race, this book will have served its purpose.

# Why Is There An Arms Race?

*"Based on Soviet writing, their strategic plans point to seizing the initiative through pre-emptive attack."*

# The Soviets Threaten World Peace

U.S. Department of Defense

In late 1981, the Department of Defense (DOD) published a 99 page book titled *Soviet Military Power*. The book consists of information taken from briefings given to the NATO Ministers of Defense and contains extensive charts, color illustrations and text, describing in great detail the growth of Soviet military power and nuclear capability. The following viewpoint, excerpted from the book, presents the claim that the U.S.S.R. has challenged the West with its massive arms buildup which is designed to project Soviet power and influence abroad. The DOD further claims that the Soviets are the aggressors in the arms race and that the U.S. is merely responding to that challenge of necessity.

Consider the following questions while reading:

1. According to the Department of Defense, why are the Soviets building up their military forces?
2. How many intercontinental ballistic missiles do the Soviets possess?
3. Why do Soviet strategic plans call for a pre-emptive attack, in the view of the Department of Defense?

Department of Defense, *Soviet Military Power*, 1981. See complete citation and ordering information on page 155.

The Soviet Armed Forces today number more than 4.8 million men. For the past quarter century, we have witnessed the continuing growth of Soviet military power at a pace that shows no signs of slackening in the future.

All elements of the Soviet Armed Forces — the Strategic Rocket Forces, the Ground Forces of the Army, the Air Forces, the Navy and the Air Defense Forces — continue to modernize with an unending flow of new weapons systems, tanks, missiles, ships, artillery and aircraft. The Soviet defense budget continues to grow to fund this force buildup, to fund the projection of Soviet power far from Soviet shores and to fund Soviet use of proxy forces to support revolutionary factions and conflict in an increasing threat to international stability...

## The Facts are Stark

The Soviet Ground Forces have grown to more than 180 divisions — motorized rifle divisions, tank divisions and airborne divisions — stationed in Eastern Europe, in the USSR, in Mongolia, and in combat in Afghanistan. Soviet Ground Forces have achieved the capacity for extended intensive combat in the Central Region of Europe.

The Soviets have fielded 50,000 tanks and 20,000 artillery pieces. The Soviet divisions are being equipped with the newer, faster, better armored T-64 and T-72 tanks. Some artillery units, organic to each division, include new, heavy mobile artillery, multiple rocket launchers and self-propelled, armored 122-mm and 152-mm guns.

More than 5,200 helicopters are available to the Soviet Armed Forces, including increasing numbers of Mi-8 and Mi-24 helicopter gunships used in direct support of ground forces on the battlefield.

More than 3,500 Soviet and Warsaw Pact tactical bombers and fighter aircraft are located in Eastern Europe alone. In each of the last eight years, the Soviets.have produced more than 1,000 fighter aircraft.

Against Western Europe, China and Japan, the Soviets are adding constantly to deliverable nuclear warheads, with the number of launchers growing, with some 250 mobile, SS-20 Intermediate Range Ballistic Missile launchers in the field, and with three nuclear warheads on each SS-20 missile.

## Priority for Missiles

The Soviets continue to give high priority to the modernization of their Intercontinental Ballistic Missile (ICBM) force and their Submarine Launched Ballistic Missile (SLBM) force stressing increased accuracy and greater warhead throw-weight. The Soviet intercontinental strategic arsenal includes 7,000 nuclear warheads, with 1,398 ICBM launchers, 950

SLBM launchers and 156 long-range bombers. This does not include some 150 nuclear-capable BACKFIRE bombers.

The Soviets have eight classes of submarines and eight classes of major surface warships, including nuclear-powered cruisers and new aircraft carriers, presently under construction. This growing naval force emerging from large, modern shipyards is designed to support sustained operations in remote areas in order to project Soviet power around the world.

The Soviet Air Defense Forces man 10,000 surface-to-air missile launchers at 1,000 fixed missile sites across the Soviet Union.

The growth of the Soviet Armed Forces is made possible by the USSR's military production base which continues to grow at the expense of all other components of the Soviet economy. There are 135 major military industrial plants now operating in the Soviet Union with over 40 million square meters in floor space, a 34 percent increase since 1970. In 1980, these plants produced more than 150 different types of weapons systems for Soviet forces and for export to client states and developing countries.

Today, the Soviets have more than 85,000 men fighting in Afghanistan. Soviet naval forces are deployed in the major oceans of the world. The USSR is gaining increased access to military facilities and is supporting proxy conflicts in Africa, Southwest Asia, Southeast Asia and the Western hemisphere.

## Soviet Military Machine

There is nothing hypothetical about the Soviet military machine. Its expansion, modernization, and contribution to projection of power beyond Soviet boundaries are obvious.

A clear understanding of Soviet Armed Forces, their doctrine, their capabilities, their strengths and their weaknesses is essential to the shaping and maintenance of effective U.S. and Allied Armed Forces.

The greatest defense forces in the world are those of free people in free nations well informed as to the challenge they face, firmly united in their resolve to provide fully for the common defense, thereby deterring aggression and safeguarding the security of the world's democracies...

## Strategic Rocket Force

The Strategic Rocket Force (SRF), the largest missile force in the world, controls all Soviet military units in the Soviet Union equipped with ICBMs, IRBMs and MRBMs. The mission of the SRF is to destroy an enemy's means of nuclear attack, military-industrial production facilities, civil and military command and control capabilities and logistics and transport facilities. The SRF's secondary mission is to support tactical

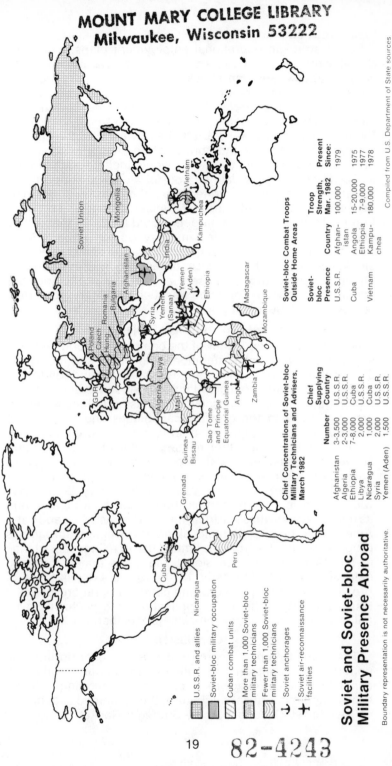

Soviet and Soviet-bloc Military Presence Abroad

joint forces and naval fleets.

Soviet strategic operational employment plans, based on Soviet writings, point to seizing the initiative through pre-emptive attack. Such an attack would effectively reduce the impact of a retaliatory strike, limiting damage to the USSR. While this is the preferred Soviet scenario, the Soviets also have the capability to launch on tactical warning if necessary. Regardless of how a war started, the Soviets view the nuclear forces and command and control of an enemy as their first priority targeting objectives. This would include such targets as ICBM launch silos, launch control facilities, support and maintenance facilities, strategic bomber bases, submarine berths and loading facilities and nuclear storage and production facilities. Priority two targets would be those that would negate the ability to project military power abroad. Such targets would include depots, transportation centers, military stockpiles, conventional force bases and training centers. Other targets would be those that limit the capacity of the enemy to conduct a protracted war such as military industries, refineries and electrical power plants...

## Soviet Global Power Projection

As self-designated leader of the communist world and as a superpower with global ambitions, the USSR and its expansionist efforts abroad are targeted at spreading and solidifying USSR political, economic and military influence and drawing nations into its orbit...Moscow's increasing boldness can be linked directly to the growing capabilities and utility of its military forces, applied in a pragmatic, coordinated and flexible manner with other military, political, economic and subversive measures to influence world events. The USSR's enhanced confidence in its capabilities to project power through a variety of military and non-military means has widened Soviet options and has been a key factor underlying its increased activities in Africa, the Middle East, Asia and Latin America. In the military realm alone, involvement abroad has progressed steadily from the limited use of military assistance in the 1950s, to the occasional use of its armed forces in defensive roles in the early 1970s, to the extensive use of proxies in advisory positions and combat operations over the last five years, to the direct application of large-scale Soviet military force in Afghanistan since December 1979...

## Conclusion

The Soviet Union's research and development priorities and continued expansion of military industrial production capabilities are keyed to supporting continuing military growth and modernization. In turn, the combined capabilities of the Soviet Ground Forces, Strategic Rocket Forces, Air

## The Threat to Europe

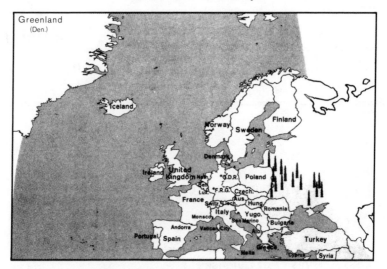

As the number of SS-20 missile launch sites in the Western USSR continues to grow, the Soviets intensify their tactical nuclear strike capability specifically targeted against Western Europe — SS-20 range and coverage extend beyond the shaded area.

Forces, Air Defense Forces and Navy are keyed to assisting the projection of Soviet power abroad and the spreading and solidifying of the Soviet Union's political, economic and military influence around the world. This is the challenge we face.

*"The Pentagon's strategic plans focus on striking the first, pre-emptive blow."*

# The Americans Threaten World Peace

U.S.S.R. Ministry of Defense

Early in 1982, the U.S.S.R. Ministry of Defense responded to *Soviet Military Power* with a publication of its own, *Whence the Threat to Peace*. The following viewpoint, which is excerpted from the Soviet book, charges that *Soviet Military Power* lacks objectivity, contains gross exaggerations and is filled with "trumped-up" claims. It points out that while the Soviet Union has military contingents in the territory of only some of its East European allies and in neighboring Mongolia and Afghanistan, U.S. military units are deployed in dozens of countries. It continues by stating that there are more than 1,500 U.S. military installations and bases overseas, chiefly in the proximity of Soviet borders. Thus, the book concludes, the United States is the aggressor in the arms race and its actions seriously threaten world peace.

Consider the following questions while reading:

1. Why does the Ministry of Defense claim the Americans, not the Soviets, are the cause of the current arms race?
2. What evidence does the Ministry present to support Its claim that American foreign policy is a policy of aggression?
3. Why does this viewpoint claim that Pentagon strategy calls for a pre-emptive nuclear attack?

*Whence The Threat To Peace.* Moscow: Military Publishing House, 1982.

It is the United States that is trying to upset the prevailing military parity, the military-strategic equilibrium. That is the goal pursued by the US President in his program of comprehensive strategic arms build-up announced in October 1981.

Reagan's program extends to all the components of the strategic offensive forces, and includes deployment of M-X intercontinental ballistic missiles and new strategic bombers, construction of Trident nuclear-powered missile submarines, escalated production of various types of cruise missiles, and other projects.

So, whose is the challenge? Who has saddled the world with the arms race?...

## American Military Power

In its *Soviet Military Power* pamphlet, the US Defense Department says the Soviet Union has 1,398 ICBM launchers, 950 SLBM launchers, and 156 heavy bombers with a total payload of nearly 7,000 nuclear weapons. These figures, taken in isolation, sound impressive. But the authors of the Pentagon pamphlet make no mention of the 10,000 nuclear weapons of the US strategic offensive forces, which have 1,053 ICBM launchers, 648 SLBM launchers and more than 570 heavy bombers, plus 65 medium bombers. In addition, the United States has thousands of nuclear-capable aircraft in its forward-based forces in the proximity of Soviet territory in Europe, the Far East, and the Indian Ocean.

It should also be borne in mind that the Soviet Union is confronted not only by the United States, but also by two other Western nuclear powers, and that the threat of China's nuclear forces is, for the time being, more serious for the Soviet Union than for the United States...

## The U.S. Military Buildup

To back up the trumped-up claim of an "alarming Soviet military build-up", various deliberately exaggerated figures are cited in the West about the military expenditures of the USSR. Contrary to the facts, the public is being told that these expenditures are continuously rising. That they have really been practically the same over the recent years, is withheld.

The military budget of the United States, on the other hand, has been rising steadily from year to year. Its rate of growth in 1978-1980, and this according to official US figures, was in excess of 13 per cent, and as much as 19 per cent in 1981. And still higher growth rates of US and NATO military spending are envisaged in the years to come. In 1985 alone, the United States is planning to allocate more than 340 billion dollars for military purposes, and a total of 1.5 trillion dollars in the coming five years...

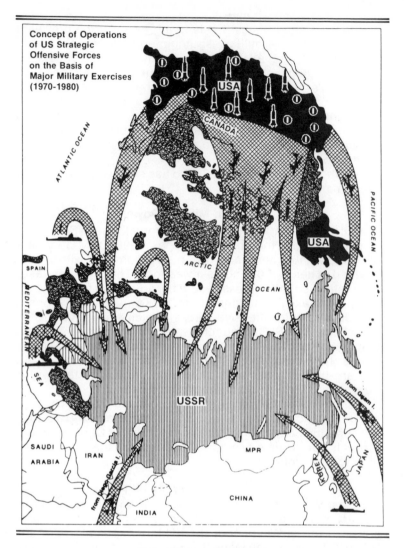

Concept of Operations of US Strategic Offensive Forces on the Basis of Major Military Exercises (1970-1980)

## U.S. Global Projection

The US Defense Department alleges that the Soviet Union seeks a "global projection of Soviet military power". Here again, however, the Pentagon is at loggerheads with the facts, and indeed with its own statements. For does it not admit that the Soviet Union has military contingents in the territory of only some of its East European allies and in neighboring Mongolia and Afghanistan, and this, moreover, strictly in conformance with treaty provisions? At the same time, US military units are deployed in dozens of countries up and down the world, and there are more than 1,500 US military installations and bases overseas, chiefly in the proximity of Soviet borders.

US nuclear-capable aircraft carriers, nuclear-powered missile submarines, and squadrons of surface warships are on continuous patrol near the shores of Europe, the Far East and in the Indian Ocean. The more than 200,000-man rapid deployment forces are ready to be moved many thousands of kilometers away from the United States of America.

## Arms to Reactionary Regimes

No less one-sided and tendentious is the account of Soviet arms shipments to developing countries. The USSR is portrayed as the biggest exporter of military hardware, though the United States accounts for nearly 45 per cent of the world arms trade. And since other NATO countries account for more than 20 per cent of the arms trade, it ought to be clear whence comes the bulk of the arms flow. It is common knowledge that US arms go to shore up reactionary and dictatorial regimes, to suppress revolutionary and national liberation movements, and to consolidate the US military presence in the recipient countries.

Like other Western propaganda publications, *Soviet Military Power* presents the fundamental principles of the foreign-policy line of the CPSU and the Soviet Government in an obviously distorted light, charging the USSR with "export of revolution", "subversive activity in other countries", and the like.

There has never been, and never will be, a single example in history that in the least confirms the fib of "Soviet export of revolution". The Communist Party of the Soviet Union acts on its conviction that revolution cannot be imposed on any country from outside: it can occur exclusively for internal reasons and conditions...

## U.S. Strategic Forces

The backbone of the US military power and nuclear potential is the *strategic offensive forces*. These include intercontinental ballistic missiles (ICBMs), strategic aircraft, and nuclear-powered ballistic missile submarines (SSBNs). That is the so-called American strategic triad.

The combat units of the US strategic offensive forces have 2,112 nuclear delivery vehicles, including 1,053 ICBM launchers, 411 bombers, and 648 ballistic missile launchers installed in 40 nuclear submarines. These can lift about 10,000 nuclear warheads of 50 kt to 10 Mt each at one launch/sortie. All in all, including reserve and mothballed heavy bombers, the US strategic offensive forces have 2,338 nuclear delivery vehicles, including 2,273 vehicles of intercontinental range, and 65 medium-range bombers specially designed for action on the European continent.

The ground-based strategic missile forces have 550 Minuteman III missile launchers, 450 Minuteman II launchers, and 53 Titan II launchers. At one launch, the US ICBMs can lift 2,153 nuclear warheads of 170 kt to 10 Mt each. These forces the politico-military leadership of the United States considers to be means of delivering a pre-emptive nuclear strike.

The sea-based strategic missile forces consist of 40 nuclear submarines armed with Trident I (216 launchers), Poseidon C-3 (304 launchers), and Polaris A-3 (128 launchers) missiles carrying over 50 per cent of total strategic nuclear force load. More than half the nuclear-powered missile submarines are on continuous combat patrol in areas ensuring delivery of nuclear strikes at targets in the interior of the Soviet Union from different directions.

Units of the strategic bomber force have 346 B-52 heavy bombers and 65 FB-111A medium bombers. The strategic bomber force is based in the continental United States and partly on Guam in the Pacific...

## US War Strategy — A Strategy of Aggression

The US Administration's bellicose foreign policy and plans to attain military superiority are reflected in Washington's new war strategy, which US Secretary of Defense Caspar Weinberger calls the strategy of direct confrontation between the USA and the USSR on a global and regional scale. This overtly aggressive strategy provides for resolute use of US military power as a tool to assert worldwide dictation by US imperialism and safeguard America's "vital interests" in many areas of the world, including access to sources of strategic raw materials and energy resources. This strategy incorporates all the provisions of the notorious Presidential Directive 59.

The principal aspect of the "direct confrontation" strategy — the most dangerous for the destinies of all mankind — is that it calls for accelerated preparation of the material facilities in the US for launching wars varying in scale and intensity.

The emphasis continues to be laid on preparations for a strategic nuclear war and the multi-purpose use of strategic forces, in accordance with the "countervailing" strategy announced in Directive 59 — from so-called limited nuclear strikes to their massive employment against the whole range of targets on Soviet territory.

A massive nuclear strike is planned in such a way as to reduce to the minimum the possibility of retaliation against the United States. The list of targets includes military installations, seats of political, state and military power, major installations of the key industries, transport and communications, and the main administrative centers in the USSR. In other words, the

Reprinted with permission from *The Daily World*.

Pentagon's strategic plans focus on striking the first, preemptive blow...

### Conclusion

Peace "from a position of strength" is what the men in Washington would like to have. These days, they are not concerned about the equality and equal security of the sides, and are bent on developing new, increasingly more destructive weapons of mass annihilation, on securing military superiority over the Soviet Union, and establishing hegemony and direct domination over other countries and nations...

The Soviet approach to this problem meets the vital interests of all peoples of the world. It means not military confrontation between states but common security. The orientation of the USSR on good-neighbourly relations and detente is not prompted by considerations of momentary advantage but by its consistent and unshakable will for peace. The USSR is not going to attack anybody and does not aim to be stronger than others. There is no weapon which it would regret discarding, provided, of course, this is done on a reciprocal basis. The Soviet Union is prepared to confirm this with actions, that is, to translate it into the language of concrete obligations in Geneva, Vienna or elsewhere...

We in the Soviet Union would like to hope that those who formulate US policy take a more realistic approach. Unrestrained intimidation of peoples with the spurious "Soviet military threat" is no longer effective. People in the West will be able to see for themselves where the threat to peace really comes from.

*"The U.S. no longer enjoys strategic nuclear superiority."*

# U.S. Must Improve Its Nuclear Deterrent

### Organization of the Joint Chiefs of Staff

The heads of the various military services of the United States, jointly comprising The Organization of the Joint Chiefs of Staff, have individually appeared at Congressional hearings during the first several months of the Reagan administration. They have given testimony in support of the Fiscal Year 1983 Defense Budget, and the overall military buildup planned for American forces for the 1980's. In January 1982, the Chiefs published a book, *United States Military Posture For FY 1983*, that amplifies their earlier testimony and statements. The following viewpoint, an excerpt from the book, claims that U.S. and allied security interests are challenged both globally and regionally by the Soviets who now have nuclear superiority.

Consider the following questions while reading:
1. Why do the Chiefs of Staff claim the Soviets have built up their military forces?
2. Why do they claim U.S. forces have declined?
3. What proof do the Chiefs present to support their claim that Soviet forces are superior to U.S. forces?
4. What program has the U.S. started to improve its forces?

The Organization of the Joint Chiefs of Staff, *United States Military Posture For FY 1983*. Washington: Superintendent of Documents, 1982.

US and allied security interests are challenged today by threats of unprecedented scope and urgency. Those threats derive from the sustained growth of Soviet military power and instabilities which confront the West in several regions of the underdeveloped world...

## The Realities

The Soviet Union remains the only nation capable of seriously threatening the US by direct military attack. This capability has increased greatly during the past decade as the Soviet Union has continued to modernize its strategic nuclear forces. The Soviets have also significantly strengthened the general purpose forces which threaten US and allied interests in Europe and Asia, and have developed force projection capabilities for operations beyond the Soviet periphery. Together with its clients and surrogates, the Soviet Union is attempting to weaken the ties between the US and its allies and displace both US and allied influence in important areas of the Third World. Thus, Soviet military power and the inclination to project that power threaten the ability of the West to protect vital interests, assist in the peaceful resolution of Third World problems, and contain situations that could lead to global conflict...

## POTENTIAL SOURCES OF CONFLICT

CONTINUING CONFRONTATION/MILITARY BUILDUP

RESOURCES-RICH REGIONS OF INSTABILITY

The potential loss of US and allied influence in any of these regions must be viewed as a matter of significant strategic concern. This concern is especially great in the case of the Middle East, where Arabian Gulf countries produce more than half the oil imported around the globe. Any significant reduction in the export of this oil or other vital resources could have enormous economic and political effects on the free world...

## Roots and Consequences of Soviet Power

The enormous growth of Soviet military power, however, presents a direct challenge to Western security and significantly complicates efforts to deal with regional instabilities. The growing Soviet capabilities have altered both the perceptions and reality of the military balance and greatly increased Soviet influence in world affairs...

Current Soviet military capabilities are the result of deliberate decisions based on a coherent strategic doctrine and pursued by the government at enormous economic cost. The Soviets have been willing to incur the drain on their economy partly because their perception of military danger to the USSR is fed by institutional pressures from within the Soviet bureaucracy. More importantly, however, the Soviets view military strength as essential to the attainment of their political objectives. Soviet military doctrine, which calls for forces structured to fight and win at any level of conflict, is based on a belief in the political efficacy of military power...

At present there is no evidence to suggest that the Soviet leaders will willingly moderate their efforts to gain military advantage. Increased Soviet prestige and freedom of action have probably confirmed their belief in the tenets of their strategic approach and reinforced their justification of the sacrifices required to implement that approach. The basic nature of Soviet military doctrine is unlikely to change. The Soviet view of the utility of clearly superior military forces is shared by political and military leaders alike and has deep historical roots. The Soviets are likely to continue to view the translation of military power into political gains as a long-term process...

## The Need for Regional and Global Perspectives

Advances in Soviet power relative to the West have resulted not only from absolute increases in Soviet capability, but also the failure of the US and its allies to keep pace. The Western democracies have been far less willing to demand economic sacrifice in peacetime and more inclined to constrain defense spending during periods of reduced tension. The Soviets have shown that they regard Western restraint as an opportunity for advantage and an invitation to subvert US and allied interests worldwide. Because it is unlikely that internal economic and social pressures alone will force the Soviet leaders to adopt a less menacing foreign policy, they must be convinced that further investments in military power can provide no net and lasting advantage...

For more than two decades the Soviet Union has pursued the steady expansion and modernization of its military forces. In addition, the Soviets have strengthened other Warsaw Pact

# U.S. AND SOVIET DEFENSE ACTIVITIES*

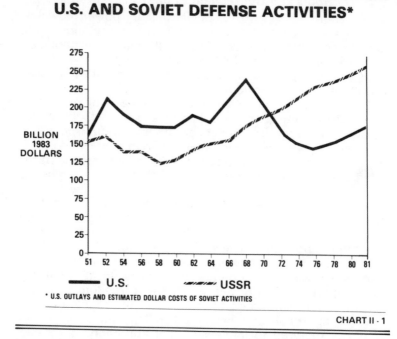

BILLION
1983
DOLLARS

━━━ **U.S.**　　╱╱╱╱ **USSR**

* U.S. OUTLAYS AND ESTIMATED DOLLAR COSTS OF SOVIET ACTIVITIES

CHART II - 1

forces and equipped Soviet clients and surrogates outside Europe as well. The failure of the US and its allies to keep pace has resulted in a growing imbalance in strategic and general purpose force capabilities...

## Comparisons Since 1970

Prior to 1970, US defense expenditures exceeded those of the Soviets. During the period 1971-1981, however, the cumulative dollar cost of Soviet defense activities has exceeded that of the US by more than 40 percent. Chart II-1 shows that as the US was winding down spending related to Vietnam, the Soviets maintained a trend of steady real growth of about three percent per year. This Soviet trend began in 1959 and is expected to continue...

## Strategic Forces

The prime objective of US strategic forces and supporting $C^3$* is deterrence of Soviet nuclear attack on the US and its allies. Deterrence depends on the assured capability and manifest will to inflict damage on the Soviet Union disproportionate to any goals that rational Soviet leaders might hope to achieve...

*$C^3$ = Command, control and communications.

## Strategic Offensive Forces

US strategic offensive forces consist of a TRIAD of ICBMs, SLBMs, and intercontinental manned bombers equipped with gravity weapons and air-launched missiles. The TRIAD of mutually supporting systems provides a mix of force characteristics for appropriate response to a number of possible Soviet attacks, complicates Soviet attack and defense planning, and insures the effectiveness of a US nuclear response.

Soviet intercontinental nuclear forces also consist of ICBMs, SLBMs, and manned bombers, but the Soviets currently place greatest emphasis on ICBMs. The Soviets have steadily increased the capability of these forces until they now exceed US forces in several measures of capability (Chart II-7 depicts the trends in numbers of US and Soviet long-range nuclear systems). The US no longer enjoys strategic nuclear superiority, and the overall effectiveness of our retaliatory capability has become increasingly uncertain.

## Sources of Deterrent Uncertainty

The increased uncertainty in the effectiveness of the US strategic deterrent has resulted from Soviet strategic force modernization and delays and deferrals of US modernization programs...The Soviets have focused primarily on modernizing their ICBM forces by deployment of new systems and by block modifications to deployed systems. These initiatives have yielded more Soviet weapons per missile, greater throw-weight, improved $C^3$, and improved weapon accuracy. As a result of these improvements — and in line with Soviet doctrinal emphasis on mass and surprise — Soviet ICBMs are now capable of destroying time-urgent targets in an initial attack.

The Soviets are also continuing to strengthen the SLBM leg of their forces. The new TYPHOON-class submarine is undergoing initial sea trials and should soon join a fleet of DELTA- and YANKEE-class ships which already far outnumber US ballistic missile submarines. The TYPHOON-class submarine, which exceeds the US TRIDENT-class in size and may rival it in technology, should become fully operational in the mid-1980s...

For their bomber force, the Soviets have retained the BEAR and BISON while continuing to add BACKFIRE. Although apparently designed primarily for peripheral missions, BACK-FIRE has sufficient range to attack the US by employing either aerial refueling or post-strike recovery in the Western Hemisphere. Long-range air-to-surface missiles (ASMs) have been deployed, and a new bomber and a new tanker are projected for the 1980s.

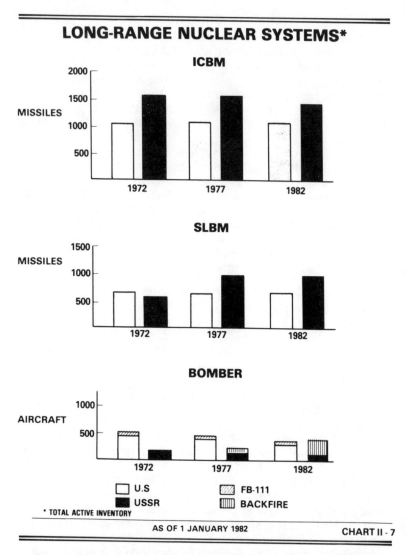

# LONG-RANGE NUCLEAR SYSTEMS*

### ICBM

MISSILES

### SLBM

MISSILES

### BOMBER

AIRCRAFT

□ U.S     ▨ FB-111
■ USSR     ⦚ BACKFIRE

* TOTAL ACTIVE INVENTORY

AS OF 1 JANUARY 1982     CHART II - 7

For a variety of reasons, US strategic force modernization efforts have not kept pace with the steady improvement of Soviet capabilities. As noted in the previous section, overall US military expenditures have been relatively limited over the past decade, largely as a result of competing priorities for national resources...

## US Strategic Force Modernization

In recognition of deficiencies in US strategic capabilities and of their underlying causes, the US has embarked on a program of strategic force modernization. The program has five segments, three of which directly concern elements of the TRIAD...The limitations of current US strategic forces did not evolve overnight; neither will their solutions.

The deployment of 100 MX missiles — each with at least ten reentry vehicles (RVs) — will address the problem of ICBM vulnerability as well as increase the number and accuracy of ICBM weapons...

Modernization of the sea-based missile force includes the TRIDENT nuclear-powered ballistic missile submarine (SSBN) program and development of an advanced SLBM, the TRIDENT II (D-5). The D-5 missile will equip the 24 launch tubes of each TRIDENT submarine, providing some increase in range and — more importantly — greater payload and accuracy for increased capability against the full spectrum of targets. The TRIDENT D-5 will be available in late 1989. In addition, nuclear-armed sea-launched cruise missiles (SLCMs) will be deployed on attack submarines beginning in FY 1984...

A variant of the B-1 bomber will become operational in 1986, with a force of 100 aircraft scheduled to be in place by the late 1980s. The new B-1B will have a much smaller radar signature than the B-52, thus enhancing bomber penetrativity well into the 1990s. In addition, an advanced technology bomber (ATB) is programmed to supplement the B-1B beginning in the early 1990s. If the threat dictates, the ATB could assume the bulk of the penetration role while the B-1, equipped with air-launched cruise missiles (ALCM), performs the stand-off mission...

### Conclusion

The steady modernization of Soviet strategic offensive and defensive capabilities has continued for more than two decades. This trend, coupled with the failure of US modernization efforts to keep pace, has resulted in the loss of US strategic nuclear superiority and increased uncertainty in US capabilities to deter both nuclear and nonnuclear conflict. The relative decline in US strategic and theater nuclear capabilities has reduced the ability of the US to deter or control lower level conflicts by the threat of nuclear escalation. To enhance the deterrence of both nonnuclear and nuclear conflict, the US must modernize the strategic TRIAD and associated $C^3$ systems and upgrade homeland defense capabilities. A sustained commitment is required to correct asymmetries in the strategic balance and create a more stable and secure deterrent.

*"There is an ingrained tendency among government officials to overstate Soviet military power."*

# U.S. Nuclear Deterrent Is Superior

Center for Defense Information

The Center for Defense Information describes itself as a non-profit, non-partisan research organization. Claiming to support a strong defense, it opposes excesses and waste in military spending and programs that increase the danger of nuclear war. CDI believes that strong social, economic, and political structures contribute equally to national security and are essential to the strength of our country. The following viewpoint, taken from an early 1982 issue of its publication, *The Defense Monitor*, concludes that American forces are superior to Soviet forces and the "window of vulnerability" described by the Department of Defense is nonexistent.

Consider the following questions while reading:

1. What evidence does CDI present to support its claim that Soviet military forces are not superior to U.S. forces?
2. Why does CDI claim we hear so many alarming statements about Soviet power?
3. Does CDI think it is possible for the Soviet Union to achieve a dominant military position in the world?

Center for Defense Information, "Soviet Military Power: Questions and Answers," *The Defense Monitor*. Volume XI, Number 1.

## Soviet Superiority?

*Question: Is the Soviet Union militarily superior to the United States?*

Answer: No. Reagan Administration officials, like their predecessors in the Carter Administration, agree that the Soviet Union does not have military superiority over the United States.

Richard Allen, then President Reagan's national security advisor, in September 1981 stated that the U.S. and the Soviet Union are equal "in almost every meaningful measure of military power."

General David Jones, Chairman of the Joint Chiefs of Staff, has stated, "We have a substantial capability today; it is not as good as it should be, but I do not foresee, in my time as Chairman of the Joint Chiefs of Staff, turning to the Secretary of Defense, the National Security Council and the President and saying, 'Do not do something because we do not have the capability.'"

Defense Secretary Caspar Weinberger has said, "We have substantial strategic strength now. There should be no misunderstanding about that."

Secretary of State Alexander Haig has maintained that "in a contemporary sense, the United States is very, very strong and very, very capable, especially in the strategic area."

The Chiefs of Staff of each of the services were asked in 1981 whether they would trade their services — its weapons, personnel, missions, entire range of capabilities, strengths and weaknesses — for its Soviet counterpart service. Each of the generals and the admiral said they would not make such a trade...

*Question: Why do we hear so many alarming claims about Soviet power?*

Answer: Military and political officials, in order to get public and Congressional support for large military budgets, believe their message must be conveyed dramatically. Our leaders naturally tend to be much more aware of and concerned about our own problems than with those of our adversaries. They tend to focus primarily on military comparisons where they feel the U.S. is deficient while ignoring comparisons where we have an advantage...

The United States, as the only truly worldwide military super-power, has demanding military objectives which constantly create tensions between available means and the ends that the U.S. seeks. We have over 500,000 military personnel stationed around the world at hundreds of bases and facilities and have assumed the mission to protect some fifty or more countries. We seek to "contain" the Soviets in countries next to the Soviet Union. As Secretary Weinberger has put it, "the key areas are close to them and far from us." Having assumed a responsibility for global containment of the Soviets, the requirement for U.S. military forces is enormous.

**At a Glance: Military Resources**
**of NATO, Warsaw Pact, & People's Republic of China**

| | NATO | Warsaw Pact | China |
|---|---|---|---|
| Population | 575,000,000 | 376,600,000 | 1,034,400,000 |
| GNP | $5,727 Billion | $2,019 Billion | $552 Billion |
| Military Spending | $241 Billion | $202 Billion | $57 Billion |
| Military Manpower | 4.9 million | 4.8 million | 4.8 million |
| Strategic Nuclear Weapons | 10,200 | 7,800 | Several hundred |
| Theater Nuclear Weapons | 21,000 | 10-15,000 | N.A. |
| Tanks | 28,000 | 63,000 | 11,600 |
| Anti-tank Missiles | 300,000+ | N.A. | N.A. |
| Other Armored Vehicles | 53,000 | 83,000 | 4,000 |
| Heavy Artillery | 15,200 | 24,000 | 18,000 |
| Combat Aircraft | 10,500 | 10,850 | 6,100 |
| Helicopters | 12,350 | 4,500 | 350 |
| Major Surface Warships | 403 | 281 | 32 |
| Attack Submarines (incl. cruise missile subs) | 224 | 298 | 104 |

N.A.—Data Not Available
Source: 1980-81 Dept. of Defense, IISS, CIA, CDI.

This makes the U.S. unique among the countries of the world in that it spends only a small percentage of its military budget for forces to defend its actual boundaries and homeland. Because of its advantageous geographic and political position, protected by oceans and bordered by friendly Canada and Mexico, the U.S. requires only small military forces to protect itself from non-nuclear attack. The U.S. spends about 10 percent of its annual military budget for continental defense. The Soviet Union, on the other hand, spends most of its military budget on defense of its huge land area and very lengthy borders where it confronts numerous adversaries. Soviet leaders cannot say about their country what General David Jones, Chairman of the Joint Chiefs of

Staff, says about the U.S.: "No one to this date or in the fore-seeable future can invade the United States."

There is an ingrained tendency among government officials to overstate Soviet military power, understate Soviet military problems, and understate U.S. and allied military power...

*Questions: Isn't the Soviet Union trying to achieve military superiority?*

Answer: There is no convincing evidence to support the proposition that the Soviet Union is trying to achieve military superiority over the United States. Soviet military forces, like those of the U.S., are both offensive and defensive in character. Their offensive forces can be used to attack the U.S. first or in retaliation to a U.S. strike against the U.S.S.R. In both cases these forces are described as deterrent forces. Most of the military effort of the Soviet Union is to defend its borders from attack by land and air forces.

Irrespective of what ultimate Soviet military objectives are, it is clearly the intention and capability of the United States, together with its main allies, to prevent the Soviet Union from achieving a dominant military position in the world.

In nuclear weapons, military spending, military technology, number of men under arms, naval forces, forces for intervention, forces in Europe, and overall world power, the Soviet Union is inferior to the alliance of powers opposing it. With growing problems in Poland and among its other military allies, the view from Moscow is far from euphoric.

## Military Spending

*Question: Does the Soviet Union outspend the United States for military forces?*

Answer: No one really knows the answer to this question. Only rough estimates can be made of the amount spent by the Soviets. The actual level of the military budget in the Soviet Union is a state secret. Soviet published budget numbers are inaccurate and far too small. Because of the vast differences between the Soviet and American economies, not even Soviet leaders have a good idea of how to compare U.S. and Soviet military budgets.

But allegations about huge military spending gaps have become central to Administration arguments for big increases in U.S. military spending. Comparisons of U.S. and Soviet spending produced by the Central Intelligence Agency (CIA) are commonly used to demonstrate the alleged inferiority of the U.S. Such political uses of CIA estimates are in fact a distortion...

Essentially, the CIA's methodology involves estimating what it would cost the U.S. to run the Soviet military system in U.S. dollars at current prices. Because prices and pay scales are very different in the Soviet Union, attempts to estimate Soviet military spending inevitably lead to erroneous conclusions. The most obvious example of this involves the cost of military personnel. Soviet conscripts receive 3.8 rubles per month, which is about $6 at official exchange rates. American volunteers are paid a minimum of $550 per month. Yet the CIA estimates assume equal pay for military personnel, which quickly translates into whopping Soviet military personnel costs because of the very large size of the Soviet Army. Ironically, each time we increase the pay of our troops, CIA estimates of Soviet military spending escalate even more...

## Winning a Nuclear War?

*Question: Do the Soviets believe that a nuclear war is winnable?*

Answer: Soviet political leaders have in recent years said they do not believe it is possible for any nation to win a nuclear war. Significantly, President Leonid Brezhnev said in October 1981:

> It is a dangerous madness to try to defeat each other in the arms race and to count on victory in nuclear war. I shall add that only he who has decided to commit suicide can start a nuclear war in the hope of emerging a victor from it. No matter what the attacker might possess, no matter what method of unleashing nuclear war he chooses, he will not attain his aims. Retribution will ensue ineluctably.

A recently published Soviet study, *The Threat to Europe*, states:

> Neither side could eventually consider itself a victor in the event of a major nuclear war between the USSR and the USA. More than a hundred million people would perish on either side, and up to three-quarters of the two countries' economic potential would be destroyed.

There is no evidence in the past fifteen years to indicate a Soviet belief in victory in a nuclear war...

## "Window of Vulnerability?"

*Question: Do our land-based missiles face a "window of vulnerability?"*

Answer: No. The Department of Defense maintains that we are facing a "window of vulnerability" because the Soviet ICBM (Intercontinental Ballistic Missile) force may soon have the capability to destroy almost all our 1052 ICBMs in a surprise attack. This scenario of possible Soviet attack on Minuteman ICBMs has never been documented by the Reagan Administration and was rejected as "far fetched" by former Defense Secretary Harold Brown. There are far too many uncertainties involved, including the possibility that the U.S. would launch its missiles before the Soviet missiles arrived. Millions of American casualties would result from such a "limited" Soviet attack against U.S. missiles. Even if many U.S. ICBM's were

# Nuclear Weapons Locations in the United States

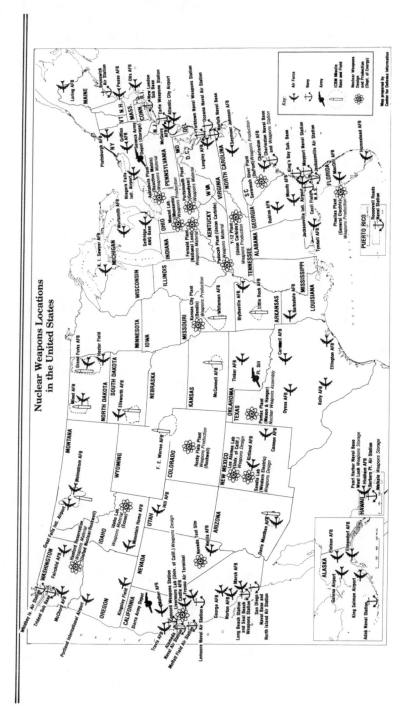

destroyed, the U.S.S.R. would have to face the prospect of devastating U.S. retaliation by thousands of nuclear weapons from U.S. bombers and submarines...

*Question: In considering an attack on the U.S., would Soviet leaders have any doubts about the U.S. retaliatory capability?*

Answer: No. The U.S. has a vast and diverse set of strategic nuclear forces. Only about 25 percent of U.S. strategic nuclear weapons are on land-based ICBMs...

Even if the Soviets can knock out most of our Minuteman ICBMs by the mid- to late-1980's, the U.S. strategic submarine fleet will have about 6000 nuclear weapons. Sixty percent of the submarine force will be at sea and will survive a surprise attack, and the 3600 weapons in the submarines will be available to destroy the Soviet Union. Invulnerable U.S. submarines can continue to attack the Soviet Union with nuclear weapons for a period of months. The U.S. will retain the capability to destroy the Soviet Union many times over.

After a Soviet attack, at least several hundred U.S. ICBMs would survive as well as some 640 SRAM missiles, gravity bombs, and about 500 air-launched cruise missiles (ALCMs) on surviving bombers. The U.S. keeps about 30 percent of its 410 long-range bombers on alert to protect them from surprise attack. The U.S. also has nuclear weapons on aircraft and missiles in Europe, Asia, and on aircraft carriers. Furthermore, the Soviets would face the prospect of attack by French, British and Chinese nuclear weapons.

*"The United States has been maintaining a level of expenditure on armaments at less than 50% of the Soviets."*

# U.S. Is Losing the Arms Race

Verne Orr

Verne Orr is currently U.S. Secretary of the Air Force. A member of the Organization of the Joint Chiefs of Staff, he is an articulate spokesperson for the Reagan Administration's program to expand America's military forces. The following viewpoint is excerpted from a speech the Secretary gave before the Los Angeles World Affairs Council on December 14, 1981. In it, he appeals to common sense, citing America's Pearl Harbor experience and admonishing that the U.S. not be caught unprepared again. He claims that the Reagan Administration has developed a "realistic and affordable" defense philosophy.

Consider the following questions while reading:

1. How does Secretary Orr relate the attack on Pearl Harbor to the arms race?
2. What evidence does the author present to support his claim of Soviet superiority over U.S. forces?
3. How does the Reagan defense policy plan to respond to Soviet superiority?

From a speech delivered by Verne Orr, U.S. Secretary of the Air Force, before the Los Angeles World Affairs Council on December 14, 1982.

Last week marked the fortieth anniversary of the attack on Pearl Harbor. In the preceding weeks and months, we were well aware that conflict existed in the world, but many people found it inconceivable that the United States would be threatened. Looking back, it is painfully clear that one principal cause of Pearl Harbor was our complacency with what had been taking place in Asia in general — and in Japan in particular — in the late 1930s and early 1940s.

Common sense tells us that we ignore the lessons of history at our nation's peril. If we are to prevent another such tragedy, the citizens of this nation, and not just those in Washington, must have an appreciation for the issues with which we are confronted in the world today...

### The Soviet Threat

Today, the Soviet Union is the only nation capable of threatening US survival by direct military attack. This capability has increased greatly during the past decade, and the result is a Soviet military machine which has a growing capacity to conduct offensive warfare anywhere on their periphery and hence to intimidate nations on or near the Eurasian landmass. Additionally, their growing force projection capability threatens to expand that capacity beyond current geographic limits. The Soviets have made conscious economic choices to reach this position, and we are today faced with countering a Soviet threat which looms larger than ever before.

Let me illustrate this point with *a few examples.*

1. Since 1960, the Soviets have increased their intercontinental nuclear delivery vehicles sixfold.
2. This year the Soviets will build about 1300 fixed wing combat aircraft. In contrast, with the Navy, we will build something less than 300 of that type of aircraft.
3. The Secretaries of the Army and Navy could tell their own stories about excessive Soviet production in ships, in submarines, in tanks, trucks and field artillery. Since 1966, the Soviets have doubled the number of artillery pieces in the field. In the same period their tank inventory grew from just over 30,000 to 50,000. The Soviets have made comparable increases in naval strength. Today the Soviet Navy operates some 377 submarines, including 180 nuclear-powered submarines compared to some 115 in the U.S. Navy. The fact is that we are being massively outbuilt by the Soviet Union in almost every area it takes to wage war.
4. It would be erroneous to assume that the Soviet's high production statistics which I have mentioned are represented by low-quality systems, that is not the case. For instance, in the area of tactical fighter aircraft, the introduction of modern aircraft such as FENCER, FITTER,

Verne Orr

FOXBAT and FLOGGER has steadily improved the offensive capabilities of Soviet Frontal Aviation since the early 70's. This modernization has changed the Soviet's tactical air forces from basically a defensive-oriented force into one which now has significantly enhanced offensive capabilities for theater warfare. These aircraft incorporate upgraded avionics and improved air-to-air missiles. The force includes sophisticated all-weather counterair fighters and ground attack aircraft. The entire counterair and about 75% of the ground attack forces are comprised of aircraft introduced in the past decade.

5. Even in space, the Soviets have continued to forge ahead rapidly. In the past ten years, the Soviets have been launching over 75 spacecraft per year — four-to-five times the number launched by the United States. We take justifiable pride in the successful flight of the Space Shuttle, but let us not overlook the fact that Young and Crippen were the first Americans in space in six years. During that same interval, the Soviets launched 20 two-man space missions and one three-man mission — a total of 43 men in space.

We are increasingly vulnerable to Soviet adventurism as long as we have the military imbalance which exists today...

## Our Inadequate Response

The United States has been maintaining a level of expenditure on armaments at less than 50% of the Soviets for at least the past four years — it has not worked. It has been said that when we build, they build; when we stop building, they build. Our defense spending is not high by historical standards.

1. Under Eisenhower, defense was 10-11 percent of GNP.
2. Under Kennedy, prior to Vietnam, it was 8 percent.
3. Projected defense budgets over the next few years do not exceed 7 percent of the GNP, less than Eisenhower or Kennedy. The question is not, "Can we afford the Reagan budget for defense?" It is, "Can we not afford the Reagan budget for defense?"

The present military buildup of the Soviet Union encourages them to undertake the type of aggression witnessed in Afghanistan. Our potential adversaries must understand that they cannot destroy us with the first strike; that our surviving forces will remain responsive under the National Command Authority; and that we are capable of denying Soviet aims.

## The Reagan Defense Philosophy

To achieve those objectives, the Reagan Administration has developed a *realistic and affordable defense philosophy* that is built upon national interests, addresses the Soviet threat and is integrated into overall national policy. Based on strength, this strategy is premised upon the idea that to survive we must have the will and the capability to meet the Soviet challenge head-on, capitalizing on the enemy's weaknesses while optimizing our own strengths.

*The nuclear element* emphasizes the development of a credible deterrent composed of survivable strategic forces possessing a war fighting capability, a reliable and survivable command and control system and a modernized strategic defense program. However, we realize that a credible deterrent cannot rely exclusively on strategic forces. We must have a strong conventional capability as well to counter conventional threats deployed against us.

*Our conventional approach* rejects the earlier perspective that nonnuclear conflict can be restricted in time and place; realizing that such conflict can spread to many theaters of operation simultaneously and will not necessarily be of short duration. Our strategy thus calls for the development of forces capable of meeting this threat, and exploiting the enemy's weaknesses.

Secretary Weinberger summarized our philosophy quite well when he said, "We must be prepared to meet Soviet military power, however it might be used. We have to be stronger than we were before because the Soviets are stronger. Otherwise we will not be able to deter the conflict we all want to avoid. And if deterrence does fail, we must be able to win to survive."

*"The Soviet threat is the big lie of the arms race."*

# The Myth of the Soviet Threat

Richard Barnet

Richard Barnet is a founder and a senior fellow of the Institute for Policy Studies in Washington, D.C. and a member of the Committee for National Security. He has taught at Yale and the University of Mexico, and during the Kennedy Administration, was an advisor in the State Department. He is the author of a number of books, including *The Lean Years: Politics in the Age of Scarcity*, *Global Reach: The Power of the Multinational Corporations* and *Roots of War*. His most recent book, *Real Security: Restoring American Power In A Dangerous Decade*, deals with the arms race and related issues. In the following viewpoint, Mr. Barnet claims that the rationale for continued American arms buildup has always been, and continues to be, a gross overstatement of "the Soviet threat".

Consider the following questions while reading:

1. Why does the author think the myth of a Soviet threat has continued for many years?
2. How does the author use the examples of the bomber gap and the missile gap to support his opinion?
3. In the author's opinion, why did the Soviets begin their arms buildup, and why do they continue?
4. What conclusion does the author come to? Do you agree?

Richard Barnet, "Lies Clearer Than Truth," *A Matter of Faith*, January 1982, p. 21. This study guide for churches was published by Sojourners, 1309 L Street N.W., Washington, D.C. 20005. Reprinted with permission.

Behind every war there is a big lie. Reality is much too ambiguous, much too complex to elicit the popular enthusiasm needed for modern mobilization...

The Soviet threat is the big lie of the arms race.

The Soviet Union does indeed pose a threat to the United States. Any power that aims thousands of nuclear warheads at our people is making and intends to make a threat. It is the same threat which the United States in more diverse and more sophisticated ways has been making against the Soviet Union for a longer time.

## The National Myth

But the Soviet threat, a national myth used as the rationale for an ever-escalating arms budget and a policy of U.S. military intervention over two generations, is something more than an official dramatization of Soviet missile strength. The Soviet threat pre-existed the Soviet missile arsenal. It is rooted in an analysis of Soviet intentions. The essence of the Soviet threat is this: The Soviet leaders, bent on world domination, will stop at nothing to defeat the United States, by bluff, if possible, by nuclear war, if necessary.

As the years go by, the characterization of the Soviet threat has changed. In the early postwar period, the Soviets were dangerous because their ideology was a powerful virus. They were, as one of our ambassadors put it, a cause rather than a country. There was nothing they were not prepared to do, even if they had nothing to do it with.

The threat salesmen of our day stand these ideas on their heads. The Soviet Union is now dangerous because its ideology has been discredited and its economy is a failure. Therefore all it has is military power, and with that power it intends to frighten us into submission.

As World War II ended, the Soviet Union lay prostrate, 73,000 cities and towns smashed, 20 million people dead. The Soviet army was in the heart of Europe, but the Soviet economy was in ruins. In order to build a Center-Right political coalition in Western Europe against the Left (until 1947 French and Italian Communists participated in the cabinets), the spectre of the Soviet invasion was raised.

Winston Churchill stated in 1950 that but for the atomic bomb in America's hands the Russian hordes would be at the English Channel. Most of the panicky public in Europe and the United States agreed. But one searches the historical record in vain for any responsible official of the West who privately shared that belief. James Forrestal, who was obsessed with the Soviet challenge, wrote in his diaries that the Soviets would not move that year — "or at any time." At the founding of NATO, John Foster Dulles, then a senator, underscored his view that the Soviets did not pose a military threat to Europe. The Joint

Chiefs of Staff testified in a similar vein.

George Kennan, the architect of the containment policy, has written that NATO was to be a "modest shield" behind which the West could restore its economy. It was not intended as a permanent standing army in the heart of Europe because there was no danger of a Soviet attack. Neither the roads nor the railroad track for a Russian blitzkrieg in Europe existed, even if the still-bleeding Soviet society could have supported one. "The image of Russia poised and yearning to attack the West and deterred only by our possession of atomic weapons was largely a creation of Western imagination, against which some of us who were familiar with Russian matters tried in vain, over the course of the years, to make our voices heard," Kennan has asserted.

---

## A Dangerous Fantasy

The standard nightmare for which our national-security strategy is designed is a Soviet attack or Soviet blackmail. If we fall short of the magic number of nuclear weapons, it is argued, Kremlin leaders may think that they would suffer "only" ten million or twenty million or fifty million casualties if they push the button; they may then conclude that running the world with the United States out of the way would be worth it.

There is nothing in Soviet behavior, history, or ideology to suggest that the model of the Soviet leader waiting by the button until the computer predicts an "acceptable" casualty level is anything but a convenient fantasy to support an unending arms race. It is said that it is a harmless fantasy, a kind of insurance policy against Armageddon. But, unlike an insurance policy, the arms race directly affects the risk. By preparing for an implausible war we make other scenarios for nuclear wars — wars by accident and miscalculation — far more probable.

Richard J. Barnet, from *Real Security: Restoring American Power In A Dangerous Decade,* 1981.

---

### The Bomber Gap

By 1955, the Soviet Union had about 350 bombers capable of delivering atomic bombs on the United States; the United States had four times the number, many located in bases close to the Soviet frontier. This was the era of the bomber gap, when Paul Nitze and many of his colleagues in the Committee on the Present Danger first began to sound the alarm.

### The Missile Gap

Then came the famous missile gap. Now Nitze and his friends accused President Eisenhower of being soft on the Russians, and John F. Kennedy campaigned for the White House in 1960 on this theme. In fact, the United States had a huge superiority in nuclear striking power. The Soviets had built very few missiles. But the new Kennedy administration ordered huge new missile programs anyway, increased the military budget 15 per cent, and "won" the eyeball-to-eyeball confrontation over the emplacement of missiles in Cuba in October, 1962.

One result of the United States "victory" was the ouster of Khrushchev, who had tried to substitute bluster and bluff for spending money on missiles, and the beginning of a serious Soviet rearmament program. It is that program which is the basis for the current hysteria about Soviet intentions.

At that time, the United States military, eager to ward off pressure for an arms moratorium, concluded that the Kremlin was resigned to being a permanent underdog. (The Pentagon has two rules for negotiating arms agreements: One is "Don't negotiate when you are behind." The other is "Why negotiate when you are ahead?") The Soviets had "lost the quantitative race," Secretary McNamara declared in 1965, "and they are not seeking to engage us in that contest."

## The Soviet Buildup

Unlike the era of the bomber gap and the missile gap, there *is* a Soviet military buildup. It has proceeded steadily since the Brezhnev era began in 1964. The rate of buildup appears to have remained the same over the years, though the pace of missile production has slowed somewhat. The current version of the big lie is that the Soviets are out to gain superiority over the U.S. The hawks warn that if present trends continue, the Soviets will have "won" the arms race and will be able to dictate surrender.

Talking about "current trends continuing" is like observing in the midst of a spring rain that if it keeps up the Empire State Building will float away. The Soviets are building to catch up. Every missile in the world not located inside the Soviet Union is aimed at the Soviet Union — those of China, Britain, France, as well as the United States. Russia is the only country in the world surrounded by hostile communist powers.

United States generals and Soviet generals genuinely disagree on how much the Soviet Union needs to catch up. What looks defensive to one looks offensive to the other. The Soviets started far behind the United States. To draw even close in nuclear striking forces their rate of production and deployment over the last 10 years would have had to be greater than that of the United States.

But the huge head start and continued commitment of the United States to the arms race still leaves this country far in the lead...

## First Strike Capability

It is the United States, not the Soviet Union, that is approaching a theoretical first-strike capability. The Soviets have most of their striking force in land-based missiles which are becoming increasingly vulnerable to our increasingly accurate warheads. Their submarine force and their bomber force are inferior copies of the United States originals. The introduction of the cruise missile, with the capability of delivering many more warheads, significantly increases the American threat for the Soviet leaders...

## The View from the Kremlin

The Kremlin's worries about the United States are not based on vague historical analogies but on painful experience. The United States participated in a military intervention in the Soviet Union after the revolution "to strangle Bolshevism in its cradle," as Winston Churchill put it. The U.S. conducted a 20-year quarantine of the Soviet Union which in part still continues.

---

## You Don't Have To Be An Expert

You don't have to be an expert to have your say on public policy. You go with whatever level of information you have. For too long, the American people, the Russian people and indeed all the peoples of this earth have been intimidated by the military technocrats on nuclear weapons policies. These fateful questions have been monopolized by the strategists and designers of military hardware. They have created their own language and developed their lunatic scenarios of such complexity that the mere citizen feels excluded from the debate.

We cannot allow this situation to continue. The basic issues of catastrophe and survival are well within the capacities of the average citizen and are generally understood. The technical details of the awful weapons are not the keys to basic policy.

Jerome Grossman, from an address, "The Medical Effects on Nuclear Weapons and Nuclear War", June 20, 1981, Chicago.

---

Looking from the Kremlin window, a Soviet leader sees the fast development of a United States-West German-Japanese-Chinese alliance, a collection of historic enemies. He sees a resurgence of anti-Soviet rhetoric and anti-Soviet politics in the United States. He may well be aware of the fact that the reappearance of the Soviet threat always coincides with the emergence of new weapons systems from the drawing boards and the renewed eagerness of one military service or another to make an addition to its bureaucratic empire. (The first wave of anti-Soviet sentiment coincided with the development of the intercontinental bomber, the second with the intercontinental missile, and the present one with the new generation of counterforce technology — MX, Trident, and the rest of the new computerized-war apparatus.) But that is small comfort...

## Conclusion

To be obsessed by the Soviet threat in a world in which more than one billion people starve, half the global work force is projected to be without a minimally paying job by the year 2000, and industrial civilization is close to collapse because political paralysis and greed have kept us from solving the energy crisis is, quite literally, to be blinded by hate.

Every time we read a statement by a general or a senator or a president that we are prepared to threaten or launch a nuclear war in order to keep the Soviet leaders from doing something we don't like, a threat to recreate a hundred Auschwitzes has been made in our name. But we are blind to it. If we do not have the clarity of moral vision to see that the Russian people cannot ever deserve a hundred Auschwitzes whatever their leaders do, then our faith rests not on reverence of God and his world but on power fantasies and fear.

The characteristic of sin is confusion. We become possessed by irrational fears. Our minds stop working. The Russians stop being people and become hated symbols. No one asks what motive they would have to drop bombs on us other than the fear that we were about to do it to them. There is no worldly prize worth the destruction of the world, or the Soviet Union, or the city of Minsk for that matter, and there is a good deal of evidence that the Russian leaders believe that. No one knows how many Russians would die from the radioactivity floating back from a Soviet attack on the United States.

The insanity of the arms race is underscored by the fact that even the most avid hawks do not believe in the eventualities against which we are pouring out our treasure and poisoning our spirit. It seems rather evident that the Russians, however depraved they may be, would rather trade with Western Europe than occupy a smoking and uncontrollable ruin.

This reality puts us very far from the choice with which the arms race enthusiasts taunt us: Red or Dead? But the question does at least force us to examine the values we think we are promoting by posing the threat of a hundred Auschwitzes...

The big lie behind all murder, from the random street killing, to the efficient ovens of Auschwitz, to the even more efficient hydrogen bomb, is that the victims deserve to die.

# Distinguishing Between Fact and Opinion

This activity is designed to help develop the basic reading and thinking skill of distinguishing between fact and opinion. Consider the following statement as an example. "Both the United States and the Soviet Union have nuclear weapons in their arsenals." The preceding statement is a fact which no historian or diplomat, of any nationality, would deny. But let us consider a statement which makes a judgement about the current nuclear arms race. "The aggressive foreign policy of the Soviet Union is the major cause of the arms race." Such a statement is clearly an expressed opinion. Attributing blame concerning the cause of the arms race obviously depends upon one's point of view. A citizen of the Soviet Union will view the arms race from a far different perspective than will a citizen of the United States.

When investigating controversial issues it is important that one be able to distinguish between statements of fact and statements of opinion.

The following statements are taken from the viewpoints in the first chapter of this book. Consider each statement carefully. *Mark O for any statement you feel is an opinion or interpretation of facts. Mark F for any statement you believe is a fact.*

If you are doing this activity as the member of a class or group, compare your answers with those of other class or group members. Be able to defend your answers. You may discover that others will come to different conclusions than you. Listening to the reasons others present for their answers may give you valuable insights in distinguishing between fact and opinion.

If you are reading this book alone, ask others if they agree with your answers. You too will find this interaction very valuable.

*O = opinion*
*F = fact*

_____ 1. It is the United States that is trying to upset the prevailing military parity.

_____ 2. At present there is no evidence to suggest that the Soviet leaders will willingly moderate their efforts to gain military advantage.

_____ 3. The Soviet Union remains the only nation capable of seriously threatening the U.S. by military attack.

_____ 4. The Soviet Union is attempting to weaken the ties between the U.S. and its allies.

_____ 5. There is no convincing evidence to support the proposition that the Soviet Union is trying to achieve military superiority over the United States.

_____ 6. We are today faced with countering a Soviet threat which looms larger than ever before.

_____ 7. No U.S. Chief of Staff would trade his branch of the military for its Soviet counterpart.

_____ 8. The fact is that we are being massively out-built by the Soviet Union in almost every area it takes to wage war.

_____ 9. The U.S. is the only truly worldwide military superpower.

_____ 10. The United States has been maintaining a level of expenditure on armaments at less than 50% of the Soviets.

_____ 11. The U.S. is unique among countries of the world in that it spends only a small percentage of its military budget for forces to defend its actual boundaries and homeland.

_____ 12. We are increasingly vulnerable to Soviet adventurism as long as we have the military imbalance which exists today.

_____ 13. The prime objective of U.S. strategic forces and supporting $C^3$ is deterrence of Soviet nuclear attack.

_____ 14. The Soviet Union is inferior to the alliance of powers opposing it.

_____ 15. U.S. strategic force modernization efforts have not kept pace with steady improvement of Soviet capabilities.

# Bibliography

The following list of periodical articles deals with the subject matter of this chapter.

| | |
|---|---|
| John F. Ahearne | "Why Should the United States Have Nuclear Weapons?" *New Catholic World*, March/April 1982, p. 56. |
| Christoph Bertram | "The Implications of Theater Nuclear Weapons In Europe," *Foreign Affairs*, Winter 1981/82, p. 305. |
| Hans A. Bethe | "Meaningless Superiority," *The Bulletin of the Atomic Scientists*, October 1981, p. 1. |
| Frank Blackaby | "World Arsenals 1982," *The Bulletin of the Atomic Scientists*, June/July 1982, p. 21. |
| William F. Buckley, Jr. | "Soviet Weakness?" *National Review*, March 19, 1982, p. 320. |
| Subrata N. Chakravarty | "The Day Admiral Rickover Got Radiated," *Forbes*, April 26, 1982, p. 50. |
| Henry Steele Commager | "Outmoded Assumptions," *Atlantic*, March 1982, p. 12. |
| Robert F. Drinan | "No Nuclear War Is Winnable," *New Catholic World*, May/June 1981, p. 108. |
| Lawrence S. Eagleburger | "U.S. Policy Toward the U.S.S.R., Eastern Europe, and Yugoslavia," *Department of State Bulletin*, August 1981, p. 73. |
| Mark R. Horowitz | "Coming to Terms With Doom: Some Missileaneous Thoughts," *USA Today*, July 1982, p. 19. |
| Spurgeon M. Keeny, Jr. & Wolfgang K.H. Panofsky | "Nuclear Weapons In The 1980's," *Foreign Affairs*, Winter 1981/82, p. 287. |
| Donald M. Kerr | "Preventing War: The Concept of Deterrence," *Vital Speeches of the Day*, June 15, 1982, p. 525. |
| Michael T. Klare | "The Global Arms Trade," *New Catholic World*, March/April 1982, p. 64. |
| John Lehman | "We Must Face the Facts As They Are," *Vital Speeches of the Day*, June 1, 1982, p. 488. |
| Milton Leitenberg | "The Numbers Game Or 'Who's On First?'," *The Bulletin of the Atomic Scientists*, June/July 1982, p. 27. |
| Sidney Lens | "A-Bomb Almanac," *The Nation*, April 4, 1981, p. 389. |
| Roy A. Medvedev & Zhores A. Medvedev | "A Nuclear Samizdat on America's Arms Race," *The Nation*, January 16, 1982. |
| *National Review* | "Anti-Nuclear Politics," May 14, 1982, p. 528. |

*Newsweek*                    "A Complex of Tricky Issues," April 26, 1982,
                              p. 26.

Richard Pipes                 "Reflections on the Soviet Crisis," *Time*, March
                              22, 1982, p. 50.

Ronald Reagan                 "A Crusade for Freedom: Military Strength Is A
                              Prerequisite for Peace," *Vital Speeches of The
                              Day*, July 1, 1982, p. 546.

Richard Thaxton               "The Logic of Nuclear Escalation," *The Progres-
                              sive*, February 1982, p. 18.

*Time*                        "Dangers in the Big Buildup," March 22, 1982,
                              p. 50.

                              "Thinking About the Unthinkable," March 19,
                              1982, p. 10.

# Do Nuclear Weapons Provide Security?

*"This is the real tragedy of the arms race. Every new advance has been justified in the name of security, and every new advance eventually makes Americans less secure."*

# More Arms
# Means Less Security

Jeffrey Rogers Hummel

While a graduate student of history at the University of Texas, Jeffrey Rogers Hummel wrote an article for *The Libertarian Review* (May 1981), titled "The Arms Race: Billions for Insecurity". In it, he argued that the United States is the instigator of the arms race and gives it its forward momentum. A former second lieutenant in the army and tank platoon leader, Mr. Hummel claims that the Soviet Union poses no conventional threat whatever to the United States. The following viewpoint, excerpted from the article, presents the scenario of the U.S. introducing most of the technological innovations in the arms race, forcing the Soviets to respond, with the end result being more sophisticated arms for the Soviets and less security for Americans.

Consider the following questions while reading:
1. How does this viewpoint justify the claim that the U.S. government is responsible for the arms race?
2. Why does the author claim that additional arms advancements will make us less secure?
3. How does the author suggest American safety and security be improved?

Jeffrey Rogers Hummel, "The Arms Race: Billions for Insecurity," *The Libertarian Review*, May 1981. Reprinted with permission.

Let us take a long hard look at the 35-year history of the arms race between the Soviet Union and the United States. When we do, we will discover that the United States government is responsible for instigating the arms race and giving it forward momentum. It has done so in the name of national security, and yet national security is the primary casualty of the arms race...

## The Myth of Imminent Superiority

Since the end of World War II, three key U.S. government reports — NSC 68 (1950), the Gaither Report (1960), and the "Team B" report (1976) — have predicted, incorrectly, imminent Soviet nuclear superiority over the U.S., setting off new rounds of weapons buildup by the U.S. with the Soviet Union scrambling to catch up a few years later. As the following chart shows, the U.S. has been the first to develop and deploy every major nuclear weapons technology, with the exception of the ICBM (which itself was the Soviet response to U.S. development of cruise missiles starting in 1954).

| WEAPONS SYSTEM | US | USSR |
|---|---|---|
| Atomic bomb | 1945 | 1949 |
| Long-range bomber | 1948 | 1955 |
| Thermonuclear bomb | 1952 | 1953 |
| Submarine-launched ballistic missile | 1954 | 1955 |
| Intercontinental ballistic missile (ICBM), liquid fuel | 1960 | 1957 |
| Nuclear submarine with ballistic missiles | 1960 | 1968 |
| Solid fuel ICBM | 1963 | 1968 |
| Multiple re-entry vehicle (MRV) — multiple warheads, one target | 1964 | 1972 |
| Multiple independently targeted re-entry vehicles (MIRV) — multiple warheads, multiple targets | 1970 | 1975 |

## Continual U.S. Superiority

Never once throughout the entire 35-year period has U.S. superiority been in doubt. While Soviet defense expenditures appear to remain fairly constant, U.S. spending has gone through peaks and troughs. The Korean War peak was followed by leaner years under Eisenhower. A second burst of U.S. defense efforts occurred under Kennedy and continued through the Vietnam War, while the years of detente ushered in another trough. Today, we have entered a third expansion in defense spending. During these fluctuations, the gulf between the Soviet Union and the U.S., particularly in the conventional realm, has widened or closed, but a decided U.S. advantage has remained an unaltered fixture of the arms race.

U.S. militarists are always willing to acknowledge that U.S.

Reprinted with permission from *The Daily World.*

superiority prevailed in the past. Yet with tedious regularity, they have repeated the assertion that at some point in the future, the Soviets will overtake and surpass the U.S. All of these analyses of the U.S.-Soviet balance have consistently relied upon grossly exaggerated assessments of Soviet capabilities. The "bomber gap," the "missile gap," the "AMB gap," and all the other alleged gaps in U.S. armaments have been total myths. The real gap generally turns out to favor the U.S.

### Yankee Ingenuity versus Security

Throughout the arms race, most of the technological

innovations have been introduced first by the U.S. The only exception to this rule is the ICBM. The world has been blessed with the atomic bomb, the hydrogen bomb, the jet bomber, the intercontinental bomber, the cruise missile, the ABM, the tactical nuclear weapon, the nuclear submarine carrying long-range ballistic missiles, the solid-fueled ICBM, the MRV, and the MIRV, all through the genius of Yankee ingenuity. In those few cases where the U.S. has not developed a weapon first, such weapons as the nuclear powered airplane or the inter-continental supersonic bomber, the weapon seems not to be developed at all. It is the United States which gives the arms race its forward momentum.

Each of these technological innovations, when introduced, did nothing to increase the security of the American people. The only possible exception, if it had worked, would have been the ABM. Otherwise, all these innovations convey to the U.S. government a military advantage that is useful in threatening opponents but of little value in actual defense.

Eventually, with dogged persistence, the Soviets, after a lag of one to five years, copy every U.S. innovation and deploy it in their own arsenal. The net result is that the U.S. is worse off than if it had never introduced the new weapon at all.

The initial U.S. monopoly on nuclear weapons and their deliverability, while doing very little to defend the American people, gave U.S. leaders an incredible leverage in their conduct of foreign policy. Once the Soviet Union had deliver-able nuclear weapons, however, this leverage deteriorated and the American people were much worse off. In 1960, before the U.S. instigated a missile build-up on both sides, the U.S. was subject to a nuclear attack of about 100 warheads. That was an intolerable situation, but it looks positively utopian when compared to the present world where the Soviets have over 6000 warheads, enough to target every U.S. city with a popula-tion over 2500 individuals.

### Arms Advances Make Us Less Secure

This is the real tragedy of the arms race. Every new advance has been justified in the name of security, and every new advance eventually makes Americans less secure. Nowhere else do the unintended consequences of government interven-tion produce the opposite of the desired goals with more vengeance. The arms race is a deadly demonstration of the inefficacy of government action.

Although one might think that the present balance of terror is about as bad as things can get, contemplate a future world in which the United States has deployed all of its projected, highly accurate, counterforce weapons, and the Soviets have matched U.S. capabilities, which they inevitably will do. Both sides will be capable of launching a preemptive first strike.

Both sides will be in a "use it or lose it" situation. Both sides, in order to safeguard their nuclear deterrent, will have strong incentives to move to a launch-on-warning posture, where their only problem will be deciding how to target their weapons. No situation could be better designed to insure that any world crisis will escalate to nuclear holocaust.

## Real Security

The object of national security is to protect people and to make them feel secure. But as the nation adds to its nuclear stockpile our peoples' faith in themselves and their future is sagging. President Reagan has pronounced the economy a "mess." Our education system is a shambles, a clear indication of our inability to invest in the future. The threat to life and property in the United States from crimes of violence mounts daily, and neither walls, locks, missiles, tanks, guns nor electric chairs will lift the burden of fear. Nostalgia for lost power that can never be recovered is no basis for security; the mindless accumulation of weaponry is sapping the spirit of our people. The power that can make us secure is not the power to bend other nations to our will, but the power to remake an America that is once again committed to the values for which the nation was founded — justice, opportunity, and the liberation of the human spirit.

Richard J. Barnet, *Real Security: Restoring American Power In A Dangerous Decade*, 1981.

## Conclusion

For anyone genuinely interested in the safety and security of the American people, stopping the arms race should be their highest priority. At some point, U.S. leaders must be forced to recognize that more and better armaments do not translate into improved defense. The initiative for stopping the arms race lies with the U.S. government. Military superiority, in a world of nuclear weapons, has become worse than useless; it is, in fact, totally counterproductive. U.S. leaders must be willing to give up superiority if Americans are ever going to enjoy greater security.

*"If we abandon our nuclear deterrent, there will be no second chance."*

# Nuclear Superiority Is the Key to Peace

Phyllis Schlafly

Phyllis Schlafly, in addition to being a famous adversary of the ERA movement, is the author of five books on defense and foreign policy. A member of Ronald Reagan's 1980 Defense Advisory Group, her most recent foreign policy book is *Kissinger On the Couch*, 1975. In the following viewpoint, excerpted from the January 1982 issue of *The Phyllis Schlafly Report*, Ms. Schlafly claims that American nuclear superiority is necessary for the maintenance of a secure peace. She warns the reader to respond to the growth of Soviet military power or risk another Pearl Harbor.

Consider the following questions while reading:

1. What evidence does the author present to prove that the world is a safer place when the United States has nuclear superiority?
2. Why does the author think we should increase our nuclear arsenal?
3. How does the author relate the attack on Pearl Harbor to the present situation of the arms race?

Phyllis Schlafly, "The Key to Peace: U.S. Superiority," *The Phyllis Schlafly Report,* January 1982.

The surest key to peace is for the United States to have military superiority over all other nations in the world. That is not just speculation, not merely a hope, not an untried hypothesis, but a fact proved by historical experience.

For the benefit of those too young to remember, and those who ought to remember but are blinded by their own pacifist biases, President Reagan explained one of the world's most important events. During the years when the United States "could have dominated the world with no risk to itself...when the United States had the only undamaged industrial power in the world...[when] our military might was at its peak, and we alone had the ultimate weapon — the nuclear weapon — with the unquestioned ability to deliver it anywhere in the world," America chose *not* to take one single step toward aggression, imperialism, or world domination.

Instead, as the President so eloquently described it, "the United States followed a course unique in all the history of mankind. We used our power and wealth to rebuild the war-ravaged economies of the world, including those of the nations who had been our enemies."

In all history, there is no record of any other nation holding such power in its hands and failing to use it to assert dominion over other nations and men. We proved that the peace and freedom of the world are safe when America has military superiority...

---

### *A Sacred Trust*

In our possession of this weapon, as in our possession of other new weapons, there is no threat to any nation. The world, which has seen the United States in two great recent wars, knows that full well. The possession in our hands of this new power of destruction we regard as a sacred trust. Because of our love of peace, the thoughtful people of the world know that that trust will not be violated, that it will be faithfully executed.

Harry S. Truman, Navy Day Address, October 27, 1945.

---

### Soviet Military Power

The greatest service the Reagan Administration can provide in the field of national defense is to give the American people the facts so they can make the right decisions. In order to do this, the Defense Department recently published what may be the most important government document in recent memory: *Soviet Military Power* (available at $6.50 from the Government Printing Office).

This factual and pictorial explanation of Soviet weaponry is clear enough for any citizen to understand, and it should be required reading for all Congressmen, media personnel, educators, and community leaders. It describes and lists the Soviet Union's strategic (nuclear) forces, theater (conventional) forces, armed forces personnel, resource allocation, quest for technological superiority, and global power projections.

In the past, the U.S. intelligence network and American leaders have done a miserable job of predicting Soviet intentions and of being prepared for their surprise moves. We would be a lot better off if U.S. strategic doctrine were based on Soviet military *capabilities* instead of on some U.S. official's guess about Soviet intentions. *Soviet Military Power* shows how tremendous those Soviet capabilities are.

### The Window of Vulnerability

"Are we dangerously behind the Russians?" a television reporter asked President Ronald Reagan at his California White House. To which the President replied, "I think we have been for some time."

A few days later, also from Reagan's ranch headquarters, Defense Secretary Caspar Weinberger discussed the national defense budget and why arms spending must remain high. He matter-of-factly commented, "We're way behind...we have to close the window of vulnerability."

Behind those two casually-reported statements lies the most shocking news story of our lifetime. Yet it was never reported as sensational news by the national media when it was happening, and, now that it has happened, it is treated as though it were a lesser item of stale news. It's a classic example of how the national media package the news in order to manage the thinking and direct the policies of the United States. The media decide what is important and what isn't...

Our present "window of vulnerability" was more accurately described years ago by General Arthur G. Trudeau in a far more apt metaphor. He said that we were fast becoming a "nuclear nudist colony." By that he meant that we are naked to the enemy; we have no defenses that can shoot down the Russian missiles if they come at us...

### Remember Pearl Harbor

As we observed the fortieth anniversary of Pearl Harbor last month, it must have seemed incredible to the current generation that the Japanese rulers, no matter how warlike, could ever have thought they could have defeated the great United States. Cross the Pacific with carriers and small propeller planes and tackle America with its vast resources?

But they did. They thought the United States wasn't ready for battle and didn't have the will to fight. "Enjoy your dream of peace just one more day...Hawaii, you will be caught like a rat in a trap," said Admiral I. Yamamoto's chief of staff, on the day before Pearl Harbor.

America was caught completely by surprise. We weren't ready for war, but we did have the will and the resources to get ready. As Yamamoto said ruefully, the Pearl Harbor attack awakened "the sleeping giant."...

Fortunately, the weapons of war in 1941 were slow enough that we had time to rearm. It took us four years and the lives of nearly 100,000 Americans to prove that the Japanese were wrong in believing they could defeat us.

America went to work and built a mighty war machine which defeated two powerful aggressors on two fronts and successfully defended ourselves and all our allies. That unparalleled military superiority lasted from the end of World War II in 1945 until the SALT I Agreements of 1972 under which our leaders agreed that the Soviet Union would have more offensive weapons than we have and that we would not build defensive weapons to protect our people from a missile attack.

Reprinted with permission.

Although we stopped building the kind of weapons that could reach the Soviet Union, they kept building the kinds of weapons that can reach us. On November 7, 1981, the Kremlin leaders stood on a balcony and watched their weapons rolling through Red Square to celebrate the anniversary of the Bolshevik revolution. "No nation will ever overtake the Soviet Union in military might," boasted Defense Minister Dmitri F. Ustinov.

The problem with thinking the unthinkable about a Pearl

Harbor-type attack in the 1980s is that there will be no time to get ready after a surprise attack. The only weapons that count are the ones in place when the first shot is fired.

That's why Winston Churchill's eloquent warning to the United States should be studied by all those trying to sabotage President Reagan's military budget: "Sometimes in the past we have committed the folly of throwing away our arms. Under the mercy of Providence, and at great cost and sacrifice, we have been able to recreate them when the need arose. But if we abandon our nuclear deterrent, there will be no second chance. To abandon it now would be to abandon it forever."

===

*"There is little reason to believe that increasing the funds we spend on arms will improve our security."*

===

# Arms Expenditures Weaken the U.S.

The Council on Economic Priorities

The Council on Economic Priorities (CEP) is a non-profit organization which describes itself as being established "to disseminate unbiased and detailed information on the practices of U.S. corporations...so that the American public could become aware of this impact and work to ensure corporate social responsibility." In March of 1982, CEP published a 54 page booklet, *The Costs and Consequences of Reagan's Military Buildup*, which was produced in conjunction with the International Association of Machinists and the Coalition for a New Foreign and Military Policy. In the following viewpoint, taken from the booklet, CEP outlines many negative consequences of the U.S. arms buildup, claiming our economy is damaged and national security weakened by massive military spending.

Consider the following questions while reading:

1. What major conclusion did CEP come to after comparing the economic performance of 13 major industrial nations over the past two decades?
2. What does CEP claim will be the economic consequences of the government's arms buildup?
3. How does CEP claim the current buildup compares to the Vietnam War buildup?
4. What evidence does CEP present to show how civilian spending creates more jobs than military spending?

Reprinted with permission from *The Costs and Consequences of Reagan's Military Buildup*, published in March 1982 by The Council on Economic Priorities. The booklet may be purchased for $2.50 from The Coalition For a New Foreign and Military Policy, 120 Maryland Avenue, N.E., Washington, DC 20002.

> The whole army and navy, are unproductive labourers. They are the servants of the public, and are maintained by a part of the annual produce of the industry of other people. Their service, how honorable, how useful, or how necessary soever, produces nothing for which an equal quantity of services can afterwards be procured.
>
> Adam Smith
> *The Wealth of Nations*

Since Adam Smith, economists have warned that if resources such as capital and labor are used for production of 'guns,' fewer will be available to produce 'butter.' Opportunities to create and strengthen civilian industries are sacrificed when resources are diverted to the military. This traditional economic logic has statistical support. The Council on Economic Priorities found that, when comparing the economic performance of 13 major industrial nations over the past two decades, those countries that spent a smaller share of economic output on the military generally experienced faster growth, greater investment and higher productivity increases. Those, like the United States, that carried a heavier military burden had poorer economic performance.

For years after the end of World War II, the American economy appeared capable of sustaining high arms budgets. In the last decade, however, the accumulated effects of heavy military spending — particularly from the Vietnam war — helped to slow economic growth, push inflation higher and leave many unemployed. Considering our continuing economic problems, President Reagan's proposal to undertake the largest peacetime military buildup in our history deserves careful scrutiny.

## A 1.6 Trillion Dollar Buildup

Will spending *$1.6 trillion dollars* over the next five years make us safer from military threats? The administration's buildup primarily increases the number of high technology weapons we buy but fails to redefine military policy. The sophisticated weaponry being purchased by the Pentagon is often unreliable and typically costs more than twice the initial estimate. This makes accurate budget planning difficult and decreases the funds available for training and maintenance. Decisionmaking at the Pentagon is largely controlled by a self-reinforcing network of Defense Department procurement officers, military contractors and members of Congress from defense-dependent districts — an 'iron triangle' of interlocking interest. Mismanagement alone accounts for $10 to $30 billion a year in Pentagon waste according to the President's budget director, David Stockman...

## The Economic Consequences

The economic consequences of buying more weaponry will be substantial. Jobs, investment, and economic growth will be sacrificed. Technological progress will be distorted. And social programs aimed at decreasing human suffering will be cut. The high technology sector, an industry important to future American economic growth, will be hardest hit by the arms increases. Even before the buildup, electronics and aerospace firms supplying the weapons industry were functioning close to their limits. Now the administration has called on industry to increase weapons output faster than during the Vietnam war. To produce the substantially greater number of sophisticated jet fighters and missiles the Pentagon is asking for, these companies must compete against civilian firms to obtain scarce resources such as technically skilled labor, key subcomponents and rare metals. Pitting military demands against civilian production will drive up prices as the economy recovers from the present recession, and could stifle the ability of U.S. technology firms to compete internationally.

## Guns or Butter

It is hardly news that in modern times our competitive position has declined steadily in relation to that of Germany and Japan. We are not less intelligent than the Germans and Japanese. Our raw material and energy base is not less good — indeed, it is far better. It is not clear that our workers are less diligent. Germany spends more per capita on its social services than we do; the Japanese do not spend much less. The difference is that the Germans and Japanese have been using their capital to replace old civilian plant and build new and better plant. We have been using our capital for industrially sterile military purposes. The comparison is striking.

Through the 1970s we used from 5 to 8 percent of our gross national product for military purposes. The Germans during this decade used between 3 and 4 percent — in most years about half as much as we did. The Japanese in these ten years devoted less than 1 percent of their gross national product annually to military use. In 1977, to take a fairly typical year, our military spending was $441 per capita; that of Germany was $252; the Japanese spent a mere $47 per capita. It was from the capital so saved and invested that a substantial share of the civilian capital investment came back which brought these countries to the industrial eminence that now challenges so successfully our own.

John Kenneth Galbraith, *The Bulletin of the Atomic Scientists*, June/July 1981.

Expanded military spending will not help solve our unemployment problem. Jobs created by arms production will go primarily to technically skilled personnel; few will be created for the semi-skilled workers most in need of jobs. And the regional imbalance of military spending will continue to shift employment from the older industrial regions of the northeast and midwest to the sun belt.

Social costs will also be high. The Reagan administration's budget represents the most dramatic shift of national priorities since the Second World War. By severely reducing the civilian budget, the government will drastically limit investment in job-creating areas like safe energy production, the railroads, housing and mass transit. Reductions in human service programs will add to the hardship of the nation's poorest citizens. Over 60 percent of those below the poverty line receive almost no assistance from 'social safety net' programs...

## Overloading the Economy

President Reagan plans to increase military spending by 52.8 percent between 1981 and 1986 in inflation-adjusted, constant dollars. When measured from the trough to the peak of the administration's plan, this expansion would be greater — by 6 percentage points — than the Vietnam war buildup (1965-1968), which is widely blamed for starting the inflation we are still trying to stop.

The largest budget additions will go for new weapons, rather than for personnel or for operations and maintenance. Pentagon officials are asking for major increases in procurement of jet aircraft, tactical missiles, tanks and ships. They are also expanding the buildup of nuclear forces. Authorizations for arms procurement are slated to grow by over 90 percent in constant dollars between 1980 and 1983, versus about 60 percent during the Vietnam mobilization...

Administration economists contend that we can absorb substantial new military spending this time because the recession has idled many industries and created high unemployment. Unlike Vietnam or Korea, they believe sufficient resources can be diverted to arms expansion without stimulating new inflation.[1]

Contrary to administration predictions, however, CEP expects that the production bottlenecks and federal deficits resulting from the arms buildup will create serious consequences for the economy. The fact that the economy is soft right now is not the issue. As we climb out of the recession, backlogs in key military-related industries will bid up prices in the high-technology sector. Soaring federal deficits, required to finance the buildup, will help push interest rates back to record level, squeezing out new investment.[2] These problems

1. Edward Cowan, "Spending By Military Is Defended," New York Times, May 4, 1981, p. D1.
2. Numerous economists have warned the administration of these problems. See James R. Capra, "The National Defense Budget and Its Economic Effects," Quarterly Review (New York: Federal Reserve Board of New York, Summer 1981). Gary Wenglowski et al. "Impact of Defense Buildup Underestimated," The Pocket Chartroom (New York: Goldman Sachs, June/July 1981). Bruce Carver Jackson, "Military Expenditures, Growth, and Inflation in the Seven Leading Industrial Countries" (New York: Brown Brothers Harriman & Co., July 1981). Henry Kaufman, "The Potential for Conflict in National Policies and Financial Markets" (New York: Salomon Brothers, April 1981).

"Sir, the ship just won't stay up with this bomb load an' people too, so . . . !"

could short-circuit economic revitalization and lead to renewed inflationary pressures...

## Declining Competitiveness

President Reagan has undertaken the largest sustained peacetime arms buildup in our history at a time when U.S. economic growth is lower than it has been in four decades. In large measure, American economic decline has resulted from slipping international competitiveness. Since their heyday in the 1960s, American companies have lost important segments of the auto, steel and commercial electronics markets to foreign competitors like Japan and West Germany. Aging U.S. industrial plants and equipment have become less efficient than their newer foreign counterparts. Inefficient U.S. firms pass along higher costs to consumers, fueling inflationary pressures. And American jobs are lost when the American-produced share of international and domestic markets declines.

During the 1970s, U.S. firms lost a substantial share of world manufacturing trade, dropping from about 21 to 17 percent. This decline came even after a major depreciation of the U.S. dollar that made American exports cheaper and foreign imports more expensive.[3] At home, the portion of total U.S. manufacturing sales supplied by American firms dropped more than three percent (from 96 to about 93 percent). While this decline seems small, it cost the economy roughly $125 billion in lost production and more than 2 million industrial jobs during the 1970s.[4] In key sectors, like autos, steel, farm machinery, consumer electronics and machine tools, U.S. firms have lost large shares of their domestic markets since 1960. These and other sectors, including the aircraft industry, were also big losers in the international arena.

## Military Spending Sacrifices Economic Performance

The military burden, in CEP's view, has significantly contributed to America's declining competitiveness. While not the only cause of our decreasing efficiency, economic performance has suffered because the United States devoted a larger share of its output to the military than its competitors. As a result, fewer dollars were available to modernize outdated industries and develop new products. Devoting over 20 percent of the nation's scientists and engineers to military research and production has distorted technological progress and also contributed to poor economic performance.[5]

We evaluated the effect of military spending on economic performance over the past twenty years by comparing the records of 13 advanced industrial nations: the United States, Canada, Austria, Belgium, Denmark, France, West Germany, Italy, the Netherlands, Norway, Sweden, the United Kingdom, and Japan.

The Council found that those nations spending a larger share of their gross domestic product (GDP)* on the military generally experienced slower economic growth than those which spent less. The United States, for example, devoted the

3. "The Reindustrialization of America," *Business Week*, Special Issue, June 30, 1980, p. 58.
4. "Reindustrialization," *op. cit.* p. 58.
5. Richard Dempsey and Douglas Schmude, "Occupational Impact of Defense Expenditures," *Monthly Labor Review*, Vol. 94, December, 1971.

*Gross domestic product (GDP) is preferred for international comparisons. It is the same as gross national product (GNP), except that it excludes imports and exports.

highest average percentage of GDP to the military while experiencing the *third lowest* growth rate...

How could higher military spending decrease economic growth? The most reasonable explanation is the negative relationship we found between capital investment and spending for arms. New, more efficient plants and equipment are critical to improving the competitiveness and long-term growth of U.S. industry. Yet military spending negatively correlates with fixed capital investment as a share of GDP in our comparison of 13 western industrial nations. The United States investment level ranks *last* in this comparison. CEP's results update similar findings by R. P. Smith of the University of London (1977) and Bruce Russett of Yale (1970)...

## Military Spending Costs Jobs

Like every previous government since World War II, the Reagan administration has stressed the economic benefits of defense spending, particularly its job-creating potential. Yet mounting evidence shows that jobs created by the military are at best a mixed blessing because they are highly skilled, concentrated in only a few geographic regions and less numerous than their civilian alternatives per dollar spent...

Beginning in the 1960s, research on the employment impacts of defense spending revealed substantial problems. Defense related jobs are clustered in relatively few categories and are unevenly distributed from state to state. As weapons sophistication increases, defense industries create fewer jobs per dollar spent. Military employment also carries with it a high "opportunity cost" in terms of civilian jobs foregone, social services cut, research delayed and investment "crowded out." Thus claims that the Reagan administration's military buildup will reduce unemployment should be viewed skeptically: renewed arms production will primarily employ engineers and technicians who already have a low unemployment rate.

While military spending creates jobs, almost any alternative use of the same money would create *more jobs*. If tax dollars are spent on weapons, jobs are foregone in other fields like housing, education, civilian research, energy efficiency and consumer goods. A growing body of research shows that this opportunity cost is high...

## Conclusion

Reagan's plan to "rearm America" is largely based on the assertion that the Soviet Union has spent $300 billion more on defense than the United States during the past decade.[6] This comparison, however, is not even an accurate accounting of military spending by western and eastern nations, much less

6. President Ronald Reagan, "State of the Union Message on Economic Recovery," *New York Times*, February 19, 1981, p. B8.

an assessment of the true military balance.

The United States, unlike the Soviet Union, has wealthy allies who together contribute almost as much as America itself to the common defense through NATO. On the other hand, the Soviet Union shoulders over three-quarters of the east's Warsaw Pact costs. When comparing the total expenditures of the two alliances (NATO vs. Warsaw Pact), instead of just the U.S. vs. the U.S.S.R., Reagan's conclusion is reversed. Over the past ten years the west has spent considerably more than eastern nations, even using Central Intelligence Agency figures which exaggerate Soviet spending[7]...

Although the Soviet Union has undertaken a steady buildup of military forces over the past two decades, there is little reason to believe that increasing the funds we spend on arms will improve our security given present policy and decision-making procedures. The missions assigned to many of the Pentagon's weapons are ill-defined and the price tags are exorbitant. Choices of which weapon to produce are determined by Pentagon procurement officials, military contractors and members of Congress whose careers often depend on developing new systems — whether or not they are necessary. Thus substantial waste could be eliminated from the Pentagon's budget without decreasing military capabilities.

7. See Joint Economic Committee, *Allocation of Resources in the Soviet Union and China. Part 6* (Washington: U.S. Congress, 1981).

> *"Defending the country is not free. It has its costs. But so do all other good things."*

# The Case for Increased Defense Expenditures

Committee on the Present Danger

The Committee on the Present Danger (CPD) was founded in November 1976 by 141 private citizens. Describing its function as directing attention to the unfavorable military balance between the United States and the Soviet Union, it is devoted to "the peace, security and liberty of the nation". As of November 1981 more than twenty members of CPD belonged to the Reagan Administration. President Reagan himself held membership before his election. The following viewpoint, taken from the Committee's publication *Is The Reagan Defense Program Adequate?* (March 1982), claims increased defense spending which is well managed will not burden the economy.

Consider the following questions while reading:

1. Why does this organization claim national security is such an important product?
2. What comparison is made to past defense spending to show that planned increases are not unreasonable?
3. How does the viewpoint refute the charge that defense spending is inflationary?

Committee On The Present Danger, *Is The Reagan Defense Program Adequate?* A pamphlet published in March 1982.

The most important thing to say about the economics of defense is also the simplest. Defending the country is not free. It has its costs. But so do all other good things — feeding the country, housing the country, and so on. To say that defense, like these other things, has its costs does not imply that those costs are not worthwhile.

The cost of defense is the diversion of productive resources — labor and capital — from other uses. The labor and capital that make military aircraft cannot be used to make video games. The men and women who serve in the armed forces cannot also serve in the police department. But that is true of all other good things. The men and women who raise cattle cannot also run hotels. The question in all these cases is whether the particular use of the resources is more valuable than the alternatives to which they might be put.

## National Security is a Good Product

People sometimes talk as if there were something special about expenditures for defense in that they yield no product. You cannot eat, drink, wear or ride in what we obtain for our national defense expenditures. But of course there is a product. The product is the national security. That is an extremely valuable product. Without it, most of the other products will not last for long or be worth very much.

It is possible to spend too much or too little on national defense, just as it is possible to spend too much or too little on housing, or on fire departments or on anything else. Even if it is agreed that more spending for defense yields more national security there is a point beyond which the addition to the national security is too small to be worthwhile. Also, even though less spending on national defense would leave more output available for other good purposes, there is some point beyond which reducing spending for defense is obviously too risky. The problem is to find the right point.

## We Spend Too Little Now

During World War II the United States devoted about 50 percent of its national output to the war effort. No one thought that was too much. No one now thinks anything like that is needed today. In the 1920s we spent less than one-half of one percent of our national output for defense. Hardly anyone thinks that would be adequate today. The relevant debate today is about the difference between spending 5½ percent of the GNP for defense and spending 7 percent on defense, despite the fact that the Committee on the Present Danger believes that the defense program proposed by the Administration is inadequate. In fiscal 1981 the United States spent about 5½ percent. The President proposes raising that to about 7 percent by 1985.

The choice between the 5½ percent program and the 7 percent program depends mainly on the assessment of the national security risks and of the contribution which the additional defense spending makes to the national security. (These questions are discussed in our basic paper, "Is the Reagan Defense Program Adequate?") But the choice also depends on the assessment of the cost. This aspect of the choice will be considered here.

## Our Nation's Security

The protection of this nation's security is the most solemn duty of any President: That is why I have asked for substantial increases in our defense budget — substantial but not excessive. In 1962, President Kennedy's defense budget amounted to 44 percent of the entire budget. Ours is only 29 percent. In 1962 President Kennedy's request for military spending was 8.6 percent of the Gross National Product; ours is only 6.3 percent.

The Soviet Union outspends us on defense by 50 percent — an amount equal to 15 percent of their Gross National Product. During the campaign I was asked any number of times, if I were faced with a choice of balancing the budget or restoring our national defenses, what would I do. Every time I said I would restore our defenses and every time I was applauded for giving that answer.

President Ronald Reagan before the 1982 Conservative Political Action Conference.

### Administration's Increase is Minimal

The fundamental implication of spending 1½ percent more of the GNP on defense is that we shall have available 1½ percent less of GNP for all other purposes — private consumption, private investment and nondefense expenditures of government. In real terms this means something like this: The Administration estimates that real output will rise by an average annual rate of 3.5 percent between 1981 and 1985. If the defense fraction were held constant, the output available for non-defense purposes would also rise by 3.5 percent per annum. But if the defense program rises as the Administration proposes, real output available for non-defense purposes will rise by an average annual rate of 3.2 percent. The difference between this 3.2 percent annual increase and the 3.5 percent we would have if we kept the defense share constant is the most general measure of the cost of the Administration's defense program.

The Congressional Budget Office makes a lower, and probably more realistic, estimate of the increase in real output in the next several years. But this estimate does not change the picture markedly. According to the CBO estimates, output available for non-defense purposes would rise by 2.7 percent per annum if the defense share was constant and would rise by 2.3 percent per annum with the Administration's defense program.

Even with the CBO estimate of the growth of real output, the output available for non-defense purposes would rise more rapidly between 1981 and 1985 than it did between 1977 and 1981.

There is little doubt that the direct cost of having a defense program equal to 7 percent of GNP rather than 5½ percent of GNP is small. That is, if the additional expenditure makes a significant contribution to the national security it is hard to argue that the diversion of 1½ percent of GNP to that purpose is an excessive burden on the economy...

It is helpful to look back at the last year when we had a balanced budget and compare it with the Reagan budget for 1985.

|  | 1969 actual | 1985 proposed |
|---|---|---|
|  | % of GNP | |
| Total expenditures | 20.2 | 20.9 |
| defense | 8.7 | 7.0 |
| non-defense | 11.4 | 13.8 |
| Total Receipts | 20.5 | 19.1 |
| Surplus | 0.4 | -1.7 |

There is a deficit in prospect now, even though a smaller share of GNP is to be spent for defense because a larger share is being spent for non-defense purposes and a smaller share is being collected in taxes.

To raise the revenue or cut the non-defense expenditures needed to finance the defense expansion will not be pleasant or politically easy. That is only saying in another way what was said at the outset, that defending the country is not costless. But the cost of the proposed program is not basically different from what is suggested by saying that it requires diverting an additional 1½ percent of GNP to defense.

## Defense Spending is Not Inflationary

A common concern about the defense expansion is that it may be inflationary. Of course, there is a historical connection between wars and inflations. But whether or not that is a necessary connection, there is no such connection between inflation and a defense program of the kind now proposed by the Administration. The argument here is perfectly simple. What causes inflation is an excessively rapid growth of *total* spending — public and private. If the growth of defense spending is financed in a way that brings about a slowdown in non-defense spending there will be no inflationary pressure of demand. That requires that the increase in defense spending be balanced by increased tax revenue or by a slowdown of non-defense spending or that monetary conditions be maintained which will keep the deficit from being inflationary.

In fact, most economic forecasters inside and outside the government, taking account of the proposed defense increase, predict that the inflation rate will come down during the next five years. That is perfectly consistent with what is expected of overall fiscal and monetary policy.

It is worth noting that during the Administrations of Presidents Eisenhower and Kennedy, when defense expenditures were 9 to 10 percent of GNP, there was little inflation. Also, the acceleration of inflation in the 1970s occurred while defense expenditures as a share of GNP were falling to their lowest level in thirty years...

## Conclusion

There is a large problem in managing the expansion of the defense program. It will go more efficiently, quickly and economically if it is well-managed. Decisions about the Congressional authorization and appropriations should be made promptly and contracts should be let quickly so that contractors can prepare in an orderly way. The Department of Defense should push forward with its program for expanding the list of qualified contractors and informing potential producers of future defense requirements. The Department should have authority to assist in the building of plant capacity that may not otherwise be available.

At a more general level, the effects of the defense expansion on the economy will depend on the monetary and fiscal policy that accompanies it. But the most significant thing to say is that with reasonably intelligent policy the burden of the program on the economy will not be excessive.

# Recognizing Statements That Are Provable

From various sources of information we are constantly confronted with statements and generalizations about social and moral problems. In order to think clearly about these problems, it is useful if one can make a basic distinction between statements for which evidence can be found and other statements which cannot be verified or proved because evidence is not available, or the issue is so controversial that it cannot be definitely proved.

Readers should constantly be aware that magazines, newspapers and other sources often contain statements of a controversial nature. The following activity is designed to allow experimentation with statements that are provable and those that are not.

The following statements are taken from the viewpoints in the second chapter of this book. Consider each statement carefully. *Mark P for any statement you believe is provable. Mark U for any statement you feel is unprovable because of the lack of evidence. Mark C for statements you think are too controversial to be proved to everyone's satisfaction.*

If you are doing this activity as the member of a class or group, compare your answers with those of other class or group members. Be able to defend your answers. You may discover that others will come to different conclusions than you. Listening to the reasons others present for their answers may give you valuable insights in recognizing statements that are provable.

If you are reading this book alone, ask others if they agree with your answers. You too will find this interaction very valuable.

> *P = provable*
> *U = unprovable*
> *C = too controversial*

_____ 1. The United States government is responsible for instigating the arms race and giving it its forward momentum.

_____ 2. Soviet strategic operational employment plans, based on Soviet writings, point to seizing the initiative through preemptive attack.

_____ 3. President Reagan has undertaken the largest sustained peacetime buildup in our history.

_____ 4. The Soviet Armed Forces today number more than 4.8 million men.

_____ 5. Throughout the arms race, most of the technological innovations have been introduced first by the U.S.

_____ 6. Every new advance in the arms race makes Americans less secure.

_____ 7. Defense spending that is well managed will not burden the economy.

_____ 8. The United States accounts for nearly 45 percent of the world arms trade.

_____ 9. If we abandon our nuclear deterrent there will be no second chance.

_____ 10. The peace and freedom of the world are safe when America has military superiority.

_____ 11. The initiative for stopping the arms race lies with the U.S. government.

_____ 12. Nations that spend a larger share of their gross domestic product on the military generally experience slower economic growth than those which spend less.

# Bibliography

The following list of periodical articles deals with the subject matter of this chapter.

Gordon Adams — "What Do Weapons Secure?" *The Bulletin of the Atomic Scientists*, April 1982, p. 8.

Richard Barnet — "The Search For National Security," *New Yorker*, April 27, 1982, p. 50.

V. Boikov — "Bankrolling the Pentagon," *World Press Review*, March 1981, p. 47.

Patrick J. Buchanan — "Reagan Defense Message Is: U.S. Vulnerable To Long-Time Soviet Threat," *Conservative Digest*, December 1981, p. 16.

"Terrible Weapons Have Role In Keeping Peace," *National Comment*, June 1982, p. 37.

William F. Buckley, Jr. — "Motives, Not Nuclear Weapons Themselves, Insane," *National Comment*, January 1982, p. 28.

*Conservative Digest* — "Defense Department Study Spotlights Huge Growth Of Soviet War Machine," November 1981, p. 26.

Robert DeGrasse, Jr. and William Ragen — "Megabucks for the Pentagon," *Inquiry*, April 26, 1982, p. 23.

John Kenneth Galbraith — "The Economics of the Arms Race — And After," *The Bulletin of the Atomic Scientists*, June/July 1981, p. 13.

Gary Hart — "National Security: The Dangers of Asking the Wrong Questions," *Vital Speeches of the Day*, March 1, 1982, p. 290.

Harry B. Hollins — "A Defensive Weapons System," *The Bulletin of the Atomic Scientists*, June/July 1982, p. 63.

Donald D. Holt — "A Defense Budget for the 1980's," *Fortune*, January 26, 1981, p. 52.

David C. Jones — "Perspectives On Security and Strategy In the 1980's," *Vital Speeches of the Day*, April 1, 1982, p. 354.

Harold Johnson — "Students For Peace and Security," *Conservative Digest*, June 1982, p. 10.

*Newsweek* — "Reagan's Arms Buildup," June 8, 1981, p. 28.

Hendrick Smith — "How Many Billions For Defense?" *New York Times Magazine*, November 1, 1981, p. 24.

C. Maxwell Stanley — "New Definition For National Security," *The Bulletin of the Atomic Scientists*, March 1981, p. 1.

84

| | |
|---|---|
| *Time* | "Arming the World," October 26, 1981, p. 28. |
| Caspar Weinberger | "We've Been Overspending, But Not For Defense," *U.S. News & World Report*, November 23, 1981, p. 29. |
| *World Press Review* | "The New Arms Debate," November 1981, p. 39. |

3 CHAPTER

# Are Nuclear Weapons Immoral?

*"As followers of Christ, we need to take up our cross in the nuclear age. I believe that one obvious meaning of the cross is unilateral disarmament."*

# Christianity Condemns Nuclear Weapons

Raymond G. Hunthausen

Raymond Hunthausen, the Archbishop of the Roman Catholic Archdiocese of Seattle, is perhaps the most prominent of the many Catholic bishops who in the past several months have spoken out against American possession of nuclear weapons. On June 12, 1981, before the convention of the Pacific Northwest Synod of the Lutheran Church in America, he articulated his controversial and now famous position to unilaterally disarm, based on a critical reading of the Gospel. The viewpoint that follows, excerpted from the Bishop's speech, offers a rationale that has provided a rallying point for many who oppose our nuclear weapons policy on moral grounds.

Consider the following questions while reading:

1. Why does Bishop Hunthausen think it is a sin to build a nuclear weapon?
2. What point does the author make when he reminds Christians of the Gospel's call to take up the cross and follow Jesus?
3. Where does the author ask Christians to place their security, other than nuclear arms?
4. Do you agree with Bishop Hunthausen's position?

Archbishop Raymond G. Hunthausen, *Faith and Disarmament*, a speech delivered to Pacific Northwest Synod for the Lutheran Church in America at Pacific Lutheran University in Tacoma, June 12, 1981.

I can recall vividly hearing the news of the atomic bombing of Hiroshima in 1945. I was deeply shocked. I could not then put into words the shock I felt from the news that a city of hundreds of thousands of people had been devastated by a single bomb. Hiroshima challenged my faith as a Christian in a way I am only now beginning to understand. That awful event and its successor at Nagasaki sank into my soul, as they have in fact sunk into the souls of all of us, whether we recognize it or not.

### It's a Sin to Build a Nuclear Weapon

I am sorry to say that I did not speak out against the evil of nuclear weapons until many years later. I was especially challenged on the issue by an article I read in 1976 by Jesuit Father Richard McSorley, titled "It's a Sin to Build a Nuclear Weapon." Father McSorley wrote:

> The taproot of violence in our society today is our intention to use nuclear weapons. Once we have agreed to that, all other evil is minor in comparison. Until we squarely face the question of our consent to use nuclear weapons, any hope of large scale improvement of public morality is doomed to failure.

I agree. Our willingness to destroy life everywhere on this earth, for the sake of our security as Americans, is at the root of many other terrible events in our country.

I was also challenged to speak out against nuclear armament by the nearby construction of the Trident submarine base and by the first-strike nuclear doctrine which Trident represents. The nuclear warheads fired from one Trident submarine will be able to destroy as many as 408 separate areas, each with a bomb five times more powerful than the one used at Hiroshima. One Trident submarine has the destructive equivalent of 2,040 Hiroshima bombs. Trident and other new weapons systems such as the MX and cruise missile have such extraordinary accuracy and explosive power that they can only be understood as a build-up to a first-strike capability. First-strike nuclear weapons are immoral and criminal. They benefit only arms corporations and the insane dreams of those who wish to "win" a nuclear holocaust.

I was also moved to speak out against Trident because it is being based here. We must take special responsibility for what is in our own backyard. And when crimes are being prepared in our name, we must speak plainly. I say with a deep consciousness of these words that Trident is the Auschwitz of Puget Sound.

### The Gospel Call to Peacemaking

Father McSorley's article and the local basing of Trident are what awakened me to a new sense of the Gospel call to peacemaking in the nuclear age. They brought back the shock of

Hiroshima. Since that re-awakening five years ago, I have tried to respond in both a more prayerful and more vocal way than I did in 1945. I feel the need to respond by prayer because our present crisis goes far deeper than politics. I have heard many perceptive political analyses of the nuclear situation, but their common element is despair. It is no wonder. The nuclear arms race can sum up in a few final moments the violence of tens of thousands of years, raised to an almost infinite power — a demonic reversal of the Creator's power of giving life. But politics is itself powerless to overcome the demonic in its midst. It needs another dimension. I am convinced that a way out of this terrible crisis can be discovered by our deepening in faith and prayer so that we learn to rely not on missiles for our security but on the loving care of that One who gives and sustains life. We need to return to the Gospel with open hearts to learn once again what it is to have faith.

We are told there by Our Lord: "Blessed are the peace-makers. They shall be called children of God." The Gospel calls us to be peacemakers, to practice a divine way of reconciliation. But the next beatitude in Matthew's sequence implies that peacemaking may also be blessed because the persecution which it provokes is the further way into the kingdom: "Blessed are those who are persecuted in the cause of right. Theirs is the kingdom of heaven".

To understand today the Gospel call to peacemaking, and its consequence, persecution, I want to refer especially to these words of Our Lord in Mark:

> If anyone wants to be a follower of mine, let that person renounce self and take up the cross and follow me. For anyone who wants to save one's own life will lose it; but anyone who loses one's life for my sake, and for the sake of the gospel, will save it. (Mark 8:34-35)

## The Weight of the Cross

Scripture scholars tell us that these words lie at the very heart of Mark's Gospel, in his watershed passage on the meaning of faith in Christ. The point of Jesus' teaching here is inescapable: As his followers, we cannot avoid the cross given to each one of us. I am sorry to have to remind myself and each one of you that by "the cross' Jesus was referring to the means by which the Roman Empire executed those whom it considered revolutionaries. Jesus' first call in the Gospel is to love of God and one's neighbor. But when He gives flesh to that commandment by the more specific call to the cross, I am afraid that like most of you I prefer to think in abstract terms, not in the specific context in which Our Lord lived and died. Jesus' call to the cross was a call to love God and one's neighbor in so direct a way that the authorities in power could only regard it as subversive and revolutionary. "Taking up the cross,"|"losing one's life," meant being willing to die at the hands of political authorities for the truth of the Gospel, for that love of God in which we are all one.

As followers of Christ, we need to take up our cross in the nuclear age. I believe that one obvious meaning of the cross is unilateral disarmament. Jesus' acceptance of the cross rather than the sword raised in his defense is the Gospel's statement of unilateral disarmament. We are called to follow. Our security as people of faith lies not in demonic weapons which threaten all life on earth. Our security is in a loving, caring God. We must dismantle our weapons of terror and place our reliance on God.

## Unilateral Disarmament

I am told by some that unilateral disarmament in the face of atheistic communism is insane. I find myself observing that nuclear armament by anyone is itself atheistic, and anything but sane. I am also told that the choice of unilateral disarmament is a political impossibility in this country. If so, perhaps the reason is that we have forgotten what it would be like to act out of faith. But I speak here of that choice not as a political platform — it might not win elections — but as a moral imperative for followers of Christ. A choice has been put before us: anyone who wants to save one's own life by nuclear arms will lose it; but anyone who loses one's life by giving up those arms for Jesus' sake, and for the sake of the Gospel of love, will save it.

To ask one's country to relinquish its security in arms is to encourage risk — a more reasonable risk than constant nuclear escalation, but a risk nevertheless. I am struck by how much more terrified we Americans often are by talk of disarmament than by the march to nuclear war. We whose nuclear arms terrify millions around the globe are terrified by the thought of being without them. The thought of our nation without such power feels naked. Propaganda and a particular way of life have clothed us to death. To relinquish our hold on global destruction feels like risking everything, and it is risking everything — but in a direction opposite to the way in which we now risk everything. Nuclear arms protect privilege and exploitation. Giving them up would mean our having to give up economic power over other peoples. Peace and justice go together. On the path we now follow, our economic policies toward other countries require nuclear weapons. Giving up the weapons would mean giving up more than our means of global terror. It would mean giving up the reason for such terror — our privileged place in the world.

How can such a process, of taking up the cross of nonviolence, happen in a country where our government seems paralyzed by arms corporations? In a country where many of the citizens, perhaps most of the citizens, are numbed into passivity by the very magnitude and complexity of the issue while being horrified by the prospect of nuclear holocaust? Clearly some action is demanded — some form of nonviolent resistance. Some people may choose to write to their elected representatives at the national and state level, others may choose to take part in marches, demonstrations or similar forms of protest. Obviously there are many ways that action can be taken.

### Tax Resistance as Obedience to God

I would like to share a vision of still another action that could be taken: simply this — a sizeable number of people in the State of Washington, 5,000, 10,000, ½ million people refusing to pay 50% of their taxes in nonviolent resistance to nuclear murder and suicide. I think that would be a definite step toward disarmament. Our paralyzed political process needs that catalyst of nonviolent action based on faith. We have to refuse to give incense — in our day, tax dollars — to our nuclear idol. On April 15 we can vote for unilateral disarmament with our lives. Form 1040 is the place where the Pentagon enters all of our lives, and asks our unthinking cooperation with the idol of nuclear destruction. I think the teaching of Jesus tells us to render to a nuclear-armed Caesar what that Caesar deserves — tax resistance. And to begin to render to God alone that complete trust which we now give, through our tax dollars, to a demonic form of power. Some would call what I am urging "civil disobedience." I prefer to see it as obedience to God...

## God or the Bomb?

We are Christians who now see that the nuclear arms race is more than a question of public policy. We believe that the wholesale destruction threatened by these weapons makes their possession and planned use an offense against God and humanity, no matter what the provocation or political justification. Through deliberation and prayer we have become convinced that Jesus' call to be peacemakers urgently needs to be renewed in the churches and made specific by a commitment to abolish nuclear weapons and to find a new basis of national security.

As the foundation of national security, nuclear weapons are idolatrous. As a method of defense, they are suicidal. To believe that nuclear weapons can solve international problems is the greatest illusion and the height of naivete.

The threatened nuclear annihilation of whole populations in the name of national security is an evil we can no longer accept. At stake is whether we trust in God or the bomb. We can no longer confess Jesus as Lord and depend on nuclear weapons to save us. Conversion in our day must include turning away from nuclear weapons as we turn to Jesus Christ.

The building and threatened use of nuclear weapons is a sin — against God, God's creatures, and God's creation. There is no theology or doctrine in the traditions of the church that could ever justify nuclear war. Whether one begins with pacifism or with the just war doctrine, nuclear weapons are morally unacceptable.

From *New Abolitionist Covenant*, originated by Fellowship of Reconciliation, New Call to Peacemaking, Pax Christi USA and World Peacemakers.

## Conclusion

I fully realize that many will disagree with my position on unilateral disarmament and tax resistance. I also realize that one can argue endlessly about specific tactics, but no matter how we differ on specific tactics, one thing at least is certain. We must demand over and over again that our political leaders make peace and disarmament, and not war and increased armaments, their first priority. We must demand that time and effort and money be placed first of all toward efforts to let everyone know that the United States is NOT primarily interested in being the strongest military nation on earth but in being the strongest peace advocate. We must challenge every politician who talks endlessly about building up our arms and never about efforts for peace. We must ask our people to question their government when it concentrates its efforts on shipping arms to countries which need food, when it accords the military an open checkbook while claiming that the assistance to the poor must be slashed in the name of balancing the budget, when it devotes most of its time and energy and money to developing war strategy and not peace strategy.

Creativity is always in short supply. This means that it must be used for the most valuable purposes. Yet it seems evident that most of our creative efforts are not going into peace but into war. We have too many people who begin with the premise that little can be done to arrange for a decrease in arms spending since the Soviet Union is bent on bankrupting itself on armaments no matter what we do. We have too few people who are willing to explore every possible path to decreasing armaments.

In our Catholic Archdiocese of Seattle, I have recommended to our people that we all turn more intently to the Lord this year in response to the escalation of nuclear arms, and that we do so especially by fasting and prayer on Monday of each week. That is the way, I believe, to depend on a power far greater than the hydrogen bomb. I believe that only by turning our lives around in the most fundamental ways, submitting ourselves to the infinite love of God, will we be given the vision and strength to take up the cross of nonviolence.

*"Our Judeo-Christian tradition not only allows but, at times, demands the ability and willingness to use force."*

# Nuclear Weapons Defend Judeo-Christian Civilization

John Lehman

John Lehman, currently Secretary of the U.S. Navy, directly attacks Bishop Hunthausen's position expressed in the previous viewpoint. His response was presented on March 7, 1982, at the Chapel of Four Chaplains honoring the famous four military chaplains who gave their lives in World War II. In the following viewpoint, Secretary Lehman interprets scripture differently than Bishop Hunthausen, claiming that when the Bible speaks of "peace-makers", it refers to those who are willing to sometimes use force to protect precious human values. He argues that the "fashionable pacifism" we see and hear today will lead to war, not peace.

Consider the following questions while reading:

1. Why does Secretary Lehman think Bishop Hunthausen's views belong to a religious minority?
2. How does the Secretary defend the possession of nuclear weapons?
3. Secretary Lehman claims our nation represents "the highest expressions of individual, political, and religious thought". Do you agree?
4. In your opinion, which individual suggests the best religious response to the arms race, Secretary Lehman or Bishop Hunthausen?

John Lehman, Secretary of the Navy, News Release by the Office of Assistant Secretary of Defense (Public Affairs), containing remarks made on March 7, 1982.

Today we do more than honor the memory of the great sacrifice made by these men of God, the heroic Four Chaplains. We also honor their spirit of patriotism, a spirit that sees no contradiction between serving God and serving in the defense of our nation, in time of peace or war. They knew that the great traditions of the faiths they represented have always viewed as honorable the defense of human values and freedoms — as the three altars bear silent but vigilant witness. This great spirit can be summed up in the traditional American phrase "For God and Country." It is a phrase that has always been closely tied to duty and honor.

## The Religious Majority

I believe that this spirit has been shared by the vast majority of men and women who — down through history to the current day — have dedicated their lives to God and their fellow men through religious vocation. We can be thankful that, in their time, they did not support the kind of pacifist ideology that has — most unfortunately — now captured a small and idealistic but vocal minority within the religious community. That wiser majority never called upon their countrymen to lay down their arms in the face of the totalitarian advance. Today, I am sorry to say, that call is being issued by a few of our countrymen.

They did not urge others in the clergy and the souls in their care to stop building those weapons that alone stand between freedom and slavery for our nation and its allies — weapons whose sole purpose is to defend our values and way of life. Such urging is now taking place.

## Nuclear Weapons Prevent War

Today we are told by a few religious spokesmen that even possession of nuclear arms by the United States is a grave evil. But all the evil seen in their lifetimes would pale beside the evil that our unilateral disarmament would inevitably produce in this country and throughout the world.

We are told that our effort to arm other nations so they might better resist Communist aggression is somehow immoral. I ask, where is the morality in Poland — in Afghanistan — in Ethiopia, Cambodia, Vietnam — in Hungary, Czechoslovakia, and inside the Soviet Union?

Can we expect morality — or justice — or restraint — from a Godless ideology? No, we cannot. History has proven that. What we can expect is oppression, power, and precious little mercy.

Those voices calling for unpreparedness and naked trust refer to themselves, naively I believe, as "the church of peace." What they are calling for would produce not only war — but the eventual loss of all freedoms for all mankind — religious freedom included.

Peace is not the result of unilateral disarmament. It never has been. And it never will be. Peace doesn't just happen; it must be forged. Peace must be made. That is why the Bible speaks of "peace-makers." Blessed are the peace-makers. This refers not merely to those who speak the words of peace but also — and with equal appropriateness — to those who take action to preserve peace. Even those of us who strongly agree that our Judeo-Christian tradition not only allows but, at times, demands, the ability and willingness to use force to protect our most precious human values, have not been energetic enough. We have taken too much for granted. We have stood by silently while vocal advocates of unilateral disarmament on the part of the United States have sought to capture public attention — and been lionized by the media.

**Stanley ■ By Murray Ball**

In a particularly tasteless example of this unfortunate trend, the Catholic Bishop of Seattle publicly called our new naval submarine base at Bangor, Washington "an American Auschwitz." Such an ignorant and repugnant statement illustrates how far the abuse of clerical power has been taken by a few religious leaders. There is, I believe, something deeply immoral in the use — or misuse — of sacred religious office to promulgate extremist political views.

### Disarmament Does Not Lead to Peace

I fully recognize that pacifism is an aspect of the religious tradition we honor today. But it is only one aspect of that tradition, and historically it has never held the prevailing view in determining moral questions of war and peace. In responding to criticisms on the naming of the nuclear submarine CORPUS CHRISTI, I "expressed my concern with the theme that...naval ships and even military service were considered somehow profane. I pointed out that commanders and crews of our naval vessels recognize fully that their essential mission is to keep the peace — and that it is vitally important that all Americans remember the humanistic values of peacekeeping."

What is needed today, more than ever, is a firm reaffirmation of the great religious tradition that has always subtended our willingness to defend our Judeo-Christian western values. We must realize — and remind our fellow countryman — that this fashionable pacifism we see and hear today — as well-intended as it may be — cannot and will not lead to peace. To disarm before a totalitarian aggressor does not lead to peace. More often, as history teaches, it leads to war. In the past, it lead to death camps and persecution — to a very real Auschwitz and the Gulag — to the Katyn Forest, and to the Vietnamese Boat People.

Whenever and wherever the voices that would unilaterally disarm us are heard, I am concerned as a Catholic and as a citizen that they have not understood the clear words of the Pope and his Secretary of State on this important subject.

This country must remain armed to insure peace. In this bitterly contested, turbulent world, we are both focus and rallying-point for those who would be free — and for the highest expressions of individual, political, and religious thought.

### We Must Defend American Values

America is the chief hope of Western Judeo-Christian civilization. For this reason we must have the courage to speak out and reaffirm the great religious traditions that support our determined efforts. Should we not speak out, we may wake up one morning and find we have lost a war of propaganda waged against a strong American defense, a war of ideas put forward by a zealous, uninformed, and unrepresentative minority in the name of valid religious values invalidly applied. The Learned Justice Louis Brandeis once said, "The greatest dangers to liberty lurk in insidious encroachment by men of zeal and well-meaning, but without understanding." It is our responsibility — that of each American — to speak out, and to see this danger contained. We must demonstrate that our deepest and most profound religious beliefs and values allow us to say — no... they demand that we say — that we are determined to arm our nation so that freedom will not be crushed.

When I became Secretary of the Navy I took a solemn vow to protect and defend the Constitution of the United States. My oath was given before my fellow countryman — and it was given before God. I do not take that oath lightly. And I disagree vehemently with those who would suggest that religious values should force me to follow policies of unilateral disarmament which would make mockery of the vow. I see no conflict between my duty and my religious beliefs. To the contrary — my religious beliefs provide vital inspiration to my efforts.

Today, tomorrow, and on into America's future, let us join together in reaffirming those religious traditions that alone

### *Unilateral Disarmament*

Today we are told by a few religious spokesmen that even *possession* of nuclear arms by the United States is a grave evil. But all the evil seen in their lifetimes would pale beside the evil that our unilateral disarmament would inevitably produce in this country and throughout the world.

John Lehman

give our defense efforts meaning and value — and a sense of higher purpose. Let us take pains to remind a new generation that "God and Country" is a religious as well as patriotic phrase, and that the defense of freedom is a positive and proper act in the eyes of the Almighty...

If specious argument by a few uninformed and overly idealistic religious leaders bias this process to the disfavor of national defense, the result could be grave. The current balance of power in the world is not that favorable to the interests of our nation — and the trends, given Soviet growth and adventure, are ominous. In this decade, America may well be seeing its last chance to become strong again and deter future incursions against us. I am pledged to see that we do not let this chance pass.

We Americans are proud of our freedom, of our history, and of our efforts to further self-determination throughout the world. Throughout America's two centuries, our idealism — when properly focused — has consistently provided benefit to mankind. Within this decade, America will reverse past trends that have weakened her — and will again be sufficiently strong to influence world events for the profoundly humane causes of freedom and justice.

America should also be proud of the great health and vitality of religion — of all religions — in our land. One of the keys to our national success is to remain the God-fearing and God-trusting people we have always been. "In God we trust" is not a hollow national slogan. It is, fittingly, the acknowledgement that Americans have always been profoundly aware of the ultimate origin of all their national blessings — and of the considerable kindnesses we enjoy in geography, history, resources, and the character of our people. Let it always be so.

*"These new weapons turn us all into murderers."*

# Nuclear Retaliation Is Murder

Helmut Gollwitzer

Helmut Gollwitzer is a German theologian who retired in 1975 as professor of systematics at the Free University of Berlin. He is the author of several books and articles relating biblical perspectives to social and political questions. The following viewpoint originally appeared as an essay in *Therefore Choose Life: Essays on the Nuclear Crisis*, a book published by The International Fellowship of Reconciliation in 1961. In his essay, Professor Gollwitzer presents a Christian case for renouncing the use of nuclear weapons under any circumstance.

Consider the following questions while reading:

1. What does the author cite as the "classic formulation" defending the Christian's participation in war?
2. What are CBR weapons, and how have they affected the morality of warfare?
3. Why does the author think nuclear deterrence is immoral, and those who use nuclear weapons are murderers?
4. What is the author's conclusion? Do you agree?

Shortened version of an essay reprinted with permission from *Therefore Choose Life: Essays on the Nuclear Crisis*. Alkmaar, Holland: International Fellowship of Reconciliation, 1961.

How can one obey the Christian message about loving God and one's neighbor, when one has to use force or even kill other people to maintain order and justice? This is where the conflict of conscience arises. Hitherto all the great Christian confessions have given the same answer (for different theological reasons but with the same result in practice).

## Wars in Defense of Justice

The classic formulation of this answer is found in the Declaration made by the Confessing Church of Germany at Barmen in 1934: "In the world which is not yet redeemed in which the church exists, the State has been entrusted by God with the task of maintaining justice and peace, as far as is humanly possible, by using (or threatening to use) force." It is therefore the duty of every Christian to assist the state in this task. Just as the police are essential for the maintenance of justice and peace at home, so the army is essential to maintain justice and peace outside. As long as the state uses the army to defend justice, the Christian acts rightly in helping the state as a policeman, soldier, or munitions worker, even if this involves having to kill those who threaten the country with armed force. Therefore a soldier *can* be in a state of grace.

## Rules of Warfare

But we must point out that this does not justify the use of violence unconditionally, nor participation in any war whatsoever. It related solely to certain definite cases, when the state was forced to have recourse to war in order to defend itself against unjust aggression and maintain justice. And even in such cases it was enjoined that the war must be conducted in accordance with the rules of honorable chivalrous combat: the civilian population must be protected, the destruction reduced to the minimum, the purpose being not to annihilate the enemy but to force the enemy to make peace. War had to a certain extent become humanized in Europe, thanks to recognition of the Red Cross, the protection of prisoners of war, and the prohibition of the use of gas and of dumdum bullets and the bombardment of open towns (as laid down in the Hague Conventions of 1907).

It was during World War II that a cleavage became apparent between the past efforts to humanize war and its future deterioration into complete brutality. It was clearly the last war in which the states involved still to some extent kept their pledge to fight in a civilized manner, but it had already shown signs of developing into an unrestricted war of annihilation.

The new factor in the situation due to the discovery of CBR (chemical, bacterial, and radiological, i.e., nuclear) weapons is that the government and military commanders are no longer in a position to decide whether they will wage war in accordance with international law. The new weapons have taken control of the situation. With such weapons it is impossible to conduct a war for the defense of justice, as in former times. They are suitable only for a war which tramples all justice and humanity underfoot.

It was only little by little that this truth became apparent to Christians. Theological ethics regarded the basic problem as solved: whether in certain cases a soldier can still be in a state of grace. They therefore did not ask themselves whether the development of modern technical weapons and military methods did not completely transform the nature of war to such an extent that it was high time for the church to protest. So we slid blindly into the age of total war, clinging to formulas which may have been applicable in earlier times...

## Participation in War is Now Immoral

The new weapons of mass destruction have brutalized warfare so completely that participation in it is completely incompatible with the will of God.

---

### A Call to Faithfulness

We are soberly reminded of God's command, "you shall have no other gods before me." But we have fallen away from God by joining our fellow citizens in succumbing to the idolatry of military might and power. To plan nuclear war assumes that tens of millions will die, justifiably in the name of national security. This exalts the nation above all else, including the survival of humanity.

From A Call to Faithfulness, circulated by the Sojourner Peace Ministry in Washington D.C. and signed by over 200 religious leaders from around the country.

---

The weapons which Paul, Augustine, and Luther had in mind could still be adapted to use in a war fought in defense of justice. Once the decision had been taken to apply force in the cause of justice, then the use of a rifle and a culverin was as justifiable as the use of a sword or a catapult. Although all lethal weapons are terrible in themselves, it could not be affirmed that such weapons "misused God's gifts, blasphemed against God's goodness, and betrayed man and woman who are made in God's image" any more than did the sword spoken of by Paul, in the face of the still more terrible reality of evil in the world and the need for adamant resistance to it.

The official reports and articles in the technical military periodicals today, describing the diabolical inventions of perverted science and strategy, give one the impression that they are written by lunatics. It suffices to read a few of them; they make it superfluous to give any lengthy explanations as to whether modern methods of mass destruction are different in quality from the weapons of earlier times.

By their very nature, these weapons eliminate all distinction between combatants and non-combatants. It is true that earlier types of weapons (from the axe to the bomb) could also be used against non-combatants; but that was an illegitimate way of using them; it was not determined by their very nature. The new instruments of warfare completely abolish all distinction between combatants and civilians; in fact,their very purpose is to decimate the population of the enemy country. By their very nature these weapons are blind.

## Annihilation Not Deterrence

The suppression of the distinction between combatants and civilians, which characterized the wars of the past, by the existence of new weapons which aim at destroying not only the enemy's troops but the entire population, changes also the character of deterrence, which is the purpose of armament in peacetime. Hitherto the purpose of armaments was to deter the enemy from aggression by threatening armed resistance.

The present methods of intimidation, on the other hand, are really threats to take reprisals on hostages. Intimidation by nuclear weapons is a threat to proceed to a terrible retribution: if millions of innocent citizens, adults and children, are wiped out indiscriminately, the same fate will be inflicted on the population of the enemy; it may even be undertaken as a preventive measure. This clearly means the end of that partial humanization of war which existed in the past, just as there can no longer be any mutually respected Red Cross and no code of ethics for the soldier. When soldiers are trained to massacre thousands of civilians at once, they cannot be expected to respect the life of an individual noncombatant.

## No Justice in Nuclear War

These weapons destroy all connection between war and justice, on which the analogy between war and police work was formerly based. This analogy made it quite clear that a war undertaken in defense of justice could not resort to "any methods whatsoever," any more than murderers can be menaced by "any methods whatsoever" in order to deter them from crime. If a person has kidnapped a child and threatens to murder it, the police cannot kidnap the kidnapper's own child and threaten to murder it. When Hitler announced, in January, 1939, that he intended to "liquidate" all the Jews in Europe if war were declared, the Western powers could not retaliate by threatening to kill an expatriated German for every Jew.

Certain methods and certain threats destroy the very justice which they are trying to safeguard. For threats are effective only if one is prepared to carry them out. Hence the limitations on the police, who cannot have recourse to "any methods whatsoever" as the criminal does. But they accept these limitations in the name of justice, which they exist to defend, and endeavor to be stronger than the criminal while confining themselves to legitimate methods, i.e., methods which respect the difference between guilty and innocent persons. The same applies to international relations; war can no longer be said to safeguard justice when the methods which it employs, or threatens to employ, are in themselves crimes...

## New Weapons Make Us Murderers

These new weapons turn us all into murderers in our mentality; for that is the only mentality which can produce and use such weapons. The older weapons left the choice of how they should be used, so that there was still some purpose in urging people to use them rightly; the new weapons, on the other hand, cannot be used except for indiscriminate mass murder. Anyone who uses them is forced into the mentality of a murderer.

A Christian church which recognizes its fellow persons as barriers appointed by God against our own sinful tendency to pride and self-glorification and which realizes that it is the body of Christ extending over all frontiers, a Christian church which recognizes that in the enemy camp there are also those whom God loves and who are members of the body of Christ, might still consider it possible to participate in the former struggles between combatants, owing to its own existence within the secular orders. But if the church were to participate in an atomic war of annihilation it would destroy itself spiritually, even more than externally. It must therefore make it quite clear in advance that it will refuse to take part in such a war.

## The Impossibility of Peace

Unlike any of the weapons of warfare used in the past, even including the biological and chemical weapons, atomic weapons affect future generations and vegetation of the earth. They are particularly horrible because they cause disastrous mutations in the reproductive genes. They thus perpetuate the destruction that they cause for an indefinite period: peace is rendered impossible. They are, therefore, completely unsuitable as means of achieving peace. The total destruction which they cause and their unforeseeable consequences exclude all possibility of forgiveness between nations. In the case of mass destruction, they would affect the very nature of humanity, and the biological changes wrought would be signs of a far deeper change: the fact that humankind had already lost all sense of right and wrong...

## Conclusion

Christians must face the question of what they will do when

they have to make their ultimate decisions; they must say quite openly that in such a case they cannot participate, that if an atomic war should break out they would take up arms only for police purposes, i.e., to protect human life from violence and oppression in the resulting chaos. In this way they will not allow themselves to be led astray by political interests and arguments. They will hold firm to the conviction that a policy which does not break God's commandments is bound to be the better policy in the long run.

Fear of Bolshevism must not drive us to resort to methods which do us more harm (both spiritually and physically) than any dictatorship could. They are the methods of a desperate practical godlessness. No one who has heard of the reality of God through the Gospel can compromise with them. Survival at all costs is a wickedly pagan policy. A Christian church which refuses to participate in it, and which remembers its own mission of peace in the world, will inspire fresh confidence and be a healing influence in a sick world menaced with disaster...

Christians cannot participate because the only condition under which it ever was permissible for them to think of taking up arms was in order to defend justice. But when the authorities urge a Christian to participate in these preparations for universal massacre, there is only one answer to be given: *"Si omnes, ego non."* If all consent, I refuse.

*"The Church considers the strategy of nuclear deterrence morally tolerable; not satisfactory, but tolerable."*

# Nations Must Defend Their Citizens

Terence Cardinal Cooke

Since 1968, Terence Cardinal Cooke, a cardinal in the Roman Catholic Church, has been the Archbishop of New York and Military Vicar for the United States Armed Forces, ministering to Catholic military personnel. In December 1981 the Cardinal addressed a letter to Catholic chaplains of the Armed Forces, its purpose being that of providing spiritual guidance on the issue of nuclear weapons. In the following viewpoint, excerpted from the Cardinal's letter, he presents his view of the Church's policy on nuclear deterrence. He argues that although the policy of deterrence may be less than ideal, one may support it in good conscience, for it provides at least some measure of security in an imperfect world.

Consider the following questions while reading:

1. How does Cardinal Cooke justify the possession of nuclear weapons?
2. What is his position on unilateral disarmament?
3. What does the Cardinal claim is the Catholic Church's position on nuclear arms?

Terence Cardinal Cooke, letter sent to Catholic chaplains on December 7, 1981 from the Military Vicariate, 1011 First Avenue, New York, NY 10022.

The Church has traditionally taught and continues to teach that a government has both the right and the duty to protect its people against unjust aggression. This means that it is legitimate to develop and maintain weapons systems to try to prevent war by "deterring" another nation from attacking. Very simply put, police carry guns for the same reason. Under no circumstances may a nation *start* a war, any more than police could decide to go out and shoot people to keep them from committing crimes! Popes have also pointed out that a nation may have the obligation to protect other nations, just as we have the obligation to go to the defense of a neighbor, even though a stranger, being attacked.

## Nuclear Weapons are Tolerable

Although the Church urges nations to design better ways — ideally, non-violent ways — of maintaining peace, it recognizes that as long as we have good reason to believe that another nation would be tempted to attack us if we could not retaliate, we have the right to deter attack by making it clear that we *could* retaliate. In very simple terms, this is the "strategy of deterrence" we hear so much about. It is not a desirable strategy. It can be terribly dangerous. Government leaders and peoples of all nations have a grave moral obligation to come up with alternatives. But as long as our nation is sincerely trying to work with other nations to find a better way, the Church considers the strategy of nuclear deterrence morally *tolerable;* not satisfactory, but tolerable. As a matter of fact, millions of people may be alive in the world today precisely because government leaders in various nations know that if they attacked other nations, at least on a large scale, they, themselves, could suffer tremendous losses of human life or even be destroyed.

It follows clearly that if a strategy of nuclear deterrence can be morally tolerated while a nation is sincerely trying to come up with a rational alternative, those who produce or are assigned to handle the weapons that make the strategy possible and workable can do so in good conscience. The Church *does* condemn the use of any weapons, nuclear or conventional, that would indiscriminately destroy huge numbers of innocent people, such as an entire city, or weapons that would "blow up the world". Every nation has a grave moral obligation to reduce and finally to get rid of such weapons altogether, but the Church points out that this must be done gradually, with all nations cooperating, and with prudence. The Church does *not* require, nor have the Popes of the nuclear age or the Second Vatican Council recommended, *unilateral* disarmament...

Terence Cardinal Cooke

## People Must Not Be Defenseless

A nation must ask itself every day: "How much defense is enough? How much is too much?" It is a matter of balance. All life must be considered precious, because every human being is made in God's Image. A nation must use resources to protect the unborn, the weak, the old, the helpless, the sick, the imprisoned, the homeless, the poor — those who most need the nation's protection and support. The question of how much the United States spends on military defense involves a number of technical issues about which I have no special expertise. The people at large and their elected representatives have the right and duty to question all aspects of the national budget, including allocations for defense. This is one of the great values and obligations of living in a democracy. We must be gravely concerned at all times about the needs of the poor and assure that appropriate provision is made for those needs. At the same time, we must be very careful about assuming that reductions in defense spending would automatically or completely solve such problems as poverty, hunger and disease in our nation or the world. These issues are tremendously complex and require many other changes in society before they can be adequately resolved. We must do everything we can to effect such changes and to resolve such problems, but even while engaged in efforts to do so, a nation must simultaneously defend *all* its people, the poor as well as the rich, against unjust aggression. There would be little point in a nation's spending all its resources on feeding, clothing, housing and educating the poor, and on other needs, only to leave all its people defenseless if attacked. We must remember, also, that these concerns are not the responsibilities of senior government officials alone. Every individual in uniform and every civilian directly involved in national defense, and particularly in defense industry, must be conscious of the many needs of the nation, especially the needs of the poor, and use the nation's resources responsibly, with meticulous honesty and care.

## A Superior Goal

The yearning to survive the nuclear age is obviously a natural, healthy goal. However, the goal of surviving with human rights is obviously a morally superior goal to mere survival.

Those who argue that risking the use of nuclear weapons is inherently immoral, fail to discuss the immorality of risking the imposition of life without any human rights on ourselves and future generations. We have seen several such societies in our lifetimes; they have not been fantasies in Nazi Germany, Soviet Russia, Pol Pot's Cambodia, Idi Amin's Uganda, El Salvador, and other unhappy lands.

From an unpublished essay, "On the Morality of Weapons," by John W. Gofman and Ms. Egan O'Connor.

I know that you and our people may be faced with difficult decisions in the future, and I will try to keep you appraised of the Church's position in each problem situation. I am well aware that a wide variety of opinions have been expressed by some people concerning the directions in which they think the Church should be moving. My responsibility as I see it, as your bishop, is to advise you of the official teaching of the Catholic Church...

## A House of Prayer and Peace

Almost 10 years ago I issued a "Pastoral Message for Peace" in which I urged that all of us together face the problem of war and begin to develop an instrumentality to prevent future wars. In that Pastoral I asserted what I believe just as strongly today, "that if we do not, with deliberate speed, develop the means of war-prevention and make impossible the waging of war by any nation on this earth, we run the risk of witnessing, in our own time, the very end of human history".

Therefore, as Military Vicar for Catholics and their families in the Armed Forces of the United States and Veterans Administration I am preparing to establish a *House of Prayer and Study for Peace*. It is absolutely imperative that we beg God's help in continuing prayer, if we are to solve problems beyond our mere human powers and mitigate or end the sufferings of war. At the same time, it is essential that we utilize our finest human resources of spirit and intellect, bringing together scientists, scholars and others to study and plan and pray to help the world achieve peace with justice.

# Recognizing Ethnocentrism

Ethnocentrism is the attitude or tendency of people to view their race, religion, culture, group, or nation as superior to others, and to judge others on that basis. An American, whose custom is to eat with a fork or spoon, would be making an ethnocentric statement when saying, "The Chinese custom of eating with chopsticks is stupid."

Ethnocentrism has promoted much misunderstanding and conflict. It emphasizes cultural and religious differences and the notion that one's national institutions or group's customs are superior.

Ethnocentrism limits people's ability to be objective and to learn from others. Education in the truest sense stresses the similarities of the human condition throughout the world and the basic equality and dignity of all people.

The following statements are taken from chapter three of this book. Consider each statement carefully. *Mark E for any statement you think is ethnocentric. Mark N for any statement you think is not ethnocentric. Mark U if you are undecided about any statement.*

If you are doing this activity as the member of a class or group, compare your answers with those of other class or group members. Be able to defend your answers. You may discover that others will come to different conclusions than you. Listening to the reasons others present for their answers may give you valuable insights in recognizing ethnocentric statements.

If you are reading this book alone, ask others if they agree with your answers. You too will find this interaction very valuable.

> *E = ethnocentric*
> *N = not ethnocentric*
> *U = undecided*

_____ 1. It is a sin to build a nuclear weapon.

_____ 2. I ask, where is the morality in Poland — in Afghanistan — in Ethiopia, Cambodia, Vietnam — in Hungary, Czechoslovakia, and inside the Soviet Union? Can we expect morality — or justice — or restraint — from a Godless ideology? No we cannot.

_____ 3. Our Judeo-Christian tradition not only allows but, at times, demands, the ability and willingness to use force to protect our most precious human values.

_____ 4. Christians must say quite openly that if an atomic war should break out they would take up arms only for police purposes.

_____ 5. Anyone who wants to save one's own life by nuclear arms will lose it; but anyone who loses one's life by giving up those arms for Jesus' sake, and for the sake of the Gospel of love, will save it.

_____ 6. What is needed today, more than ever, is a firm reaffirmation of the great religious tradition that has always subtended our willingness to defend our Judeo-Christian western values.

_____ 7. America is the chief hope of Western Judeo-Christian civilization.

_____ 8. We must dismantle our weapons of terror and place our reliance on God.

_____ 9. Throughout America's two centuries, our idealism — when properly focused — has consistently provided benefit to mankind.

_____ 10. One obvious meaning of the cross is unilateral disarmament.

_____ 11. Let us take pains to remind a new generation that "God and Country" is a religious as well as patriotic phrase, and that the defense of freedom is a positive and proper act in the eyes of the Almighty.

_____ 12. If the church were to participate in an atomic war of annihilation it would destroy itself spiritually, even more than externally.

_____ 13. Survival at all costs is a wickedly pagan policy.

# Bibliography

The following list of periodical articles deals with the subject matter of this chapter.

| | |
|---|---|
| Timothy Ashby | "Pacifism: A Growing Threat," *New Guard*, Summer 1982, p. 37. |
| Lloyd J. Averill | "Nuclear Morality," *The Christian Century*, April 14, 1982, p. 437. |
| John C. Bennett | "Countering the Theory of Limited Nuclear War," *The Christian Century*, January 7-14, 1982, p. 11. |
| William F. Buckley Jr. | "Before You Say No," *National Review*, May 28, 1982, p. 652. |
| | "The Sad Story of Bishop Drury," *National Review*, January 22, 1982, p. 71. |
| *Christianity Today* | "A Proposal to Tilt the Balance of Terror," April 9, 1982, p. 16. |
| John R. Connery | "The Morality of Nuclear Warpower," *America*, July 17, 1982, p. 25. |
| William Durland | "The Cost of Conscience," *Sojourners*, March 1982, p. 10. |
| Edwin Brown Firmage | "Allegiance & Stewardship," *Christianity and Crisis*, March 1, 1982, p. 49. |
| Frye Gaillard | "The Conversion of Billy Graham, *The Progressive*, August 1982, p. 26. |
| Billy Graham | "A Change of Heart," *Sojourners*, August 1979, p. 12. |
| Frederick Herzog | "Passing the Peace," *Christianity and Crisis*, March 1, 1982, p. 44. |
| Mary Evelyn Jegen | "Christian Spirituality, Disarmament and Security," *New Catholic World*, March/April 1982, p. 85. |
| John Junkerman | "Why Pray for Peace While Paying for War?" *The Progressive*, April 1981, p. 14. |
| Herman Kahn | "Thinking About Nuclear Morality," *New York Times Magazine*, June 13, 1982, p. 42. |
| Roger Mahony | "Becoming A Church of Peace Advocacy," *Christianity and Crisis*, March 1, 1982, p. 37. |
| Francis X. Meehan | "The Moral Dimensions of Disarmament," *New Catholic World*, March/April 1982, p. 68. |
| Michael Novak | "Arms and the Church," *Commentary*, March 1982, p. 37. |

Michael Novak                    "Mahonyism," *National Review*, July 9, 1982, p. 838.

                                 "Nuclear Morality," *America*, July 3, 1982, p. 5.

John B. Massen                   "An Atheist's View of the Arms Race and Nuclear War," *American Atheists*, May 1982, p. 20.

Joseph A. O'Hare                 "One Man's Primer On Nuclear Morality," *America*, July 3, 1982, p. 9.

Thomas J. Reese                  "Should We Surrender?" *America*, January 16, 1982, p. 33.

James V. Schall                  "Ecclesiastical Wars Over Peace," *National Review*, June 25, 1982, p. 757.

*Sojourners*                     "Converting To Peace," January 1982, p. 10.

George F. Will                   "Nuclear Morality," *Newsweek*, December 21, 1982, p. 84.

Walter Wink                      "Faith and Nuclear Paralysis," *The Christian Century*, March 3, 1982, p. 234.

# How Can the Arms Race Be Stopped?

> *"There are many reasons to support a halt to the nuclear arms race at this time."*

# The Case for a Nuclear Freeze

Randall Forsberg

Randall Forsberg is the founder and director of the Institute for Defense & Disarmament Studies. For seven years Ms. Forsberg worked at the Stockholm International Peace Research Institute. The author of a number of books and publications on defense and disarmament, she is the principal author of *A Call To Halt the Nuclear Arms Race* which is printed by The American Friends Service Committee. The following viewpoint, which is excerpted from "A Call To Halt", claims that because of new weapons just on the horizon, it is imperative that the arms race be stopped now. Ms. Forsberg, and the freeze movement she has helped spawn, warns that the "nuclear tripwire" will be pulled tighter if an immediate freeze is not enacted.

Consider the following questions while reading:

1. What is "nuclear warfighting" and why does this viewpoint claim it increases the likelihood of nuclear war?
2. Why do freeze advocates claim the advent of the cruise missile makes a nuclear freeze important now?
3. In addition to lessening the chances of nuclear war, what additional benefits do freeze advocates predict?

Randall Forsberg, *Call To Halt the Nuclear Arms Race*, distributed by American Friends Service Committee. 1501 Cherry Street. Philadelphia. PA 19102.

To improve national and international security, the United States and the Soviet Union should stop the nuclear arms race. Specifically, they should adopt a mutual freeze on the testing, production and deployment of nuclear weapons and of missiles and new aircraft designed primarily to deliver nuclear weapons. This is an essential, verifiable first step toward lessening the risk of nuclear war and reducing the nuclear arsenals.

The horror of a nuclear holocaust is universally acknowledged. Today, the United States and the Soviet Union possess 50,000 nuclear weapons. In half an hour, a fraction of these weapons can destroy all cities in the northern hemisphere. Yet over the next decade, the USA and USSR plan to build over 20,000 more nuclear warheads, along with a new generation of nuclear missiles and aircraft.

The weapon programs of the next decade, if not stopped, will pull the nuclear tripwire tighter...

There are many reasons to support a halt to the nuclear arms race at this time:

### Parity

There is widespread agreement that parity exists between US and Soviet nuclear forces at present.

### Avoiding "Nuclear Warfighting" Developments

The next generation US and Soviet nuclear weapons improve "nuclear warfighting" capabilities — that is, they improve the ability to knock out the enemy's forces in what is termed a "limited" nuclear exchange. Having such capabilities will undermine the sense of parity, spur further weapon developments and increase the likelihood of nuclear war in a crisis, especially if conflict with conventional weapons has started. It is of overriding importance to stop these developments.

### Stopping the MX and New Soviet ICBMs

Specifically, a freeze would prevent the deployment of new and improved Soviet ICBMs, which are expected to render US ICBMs vulnerable to preemptive attack. This would obviate the need for the costly and environmentally-destructive US mobile MX ICBM, with its counterforce capability against Soviet ICBMs. That, in turn, would avoid the pressure for the USSR to deploy its own mobile ICBMs in the 1990s.

### Stopping the Cruise Missile

The new US cruise missile, just entering production in an air-launched version and still in development in ground- and sea-launched versions, threatens to make negotiated, nationally-verified nuclear arms control far more difficult. Modern, low-flying, terrain-guided cruise missiles are relatively small and cheap and can be deployed in large numbers on virtually any launching platform: not only bombers, but also tactical aircraft, surface ships, tactical submarines, and various ground vehicles. They are easy to conceal and, unlike ICBMs, their numbers cannot be observed from satellites. If the United States continues the development and production of cruise missiles, the USSR will be likely to follow suit in 5-10 years; and quantitative limits on the two sides will be impossible to verify. A freeze would preclude this development.

Reprinted by permission of United Features Syndicate.

## Preserving European Security

A freeze would also prevent a worsening of the nuclear balance in Europe. To date, the USSR has replaced less than half of its medium-range nuclear missiles and bombers with the new SS-20 missile and Backfire bomber. The United States is planning to add hundreds of Pershing II and ground-launched cruise missiles to the forward-based nuclear systems in Europe, capable of reaching the USSR. Negotiations conducted *after* additional Soviet medium-range weapons are deployed are likely to leave Europe with more nuclear arms on both sides and with less security than it has today. It is important to freeze before the Soviet weapons grow to large numbers, increasing pressure for a US response and committing both sides to permanently higher nuclear force levels.

## Stopping the Spread of Nuclear Arms

There is a slim chance of stopping the spread of nuclear weapons if the two superpowers stop their major nuclear arms race. The freeze would help the USA and USSR meet their legal and political obligations under the Nonproliferation Treaty. It would make the renunciation of nuclear weapons by other countries somewhat more equitable and politically feasible. In addition, a US-Soviet freeze would encourage a halt in the nuclear weapon programs of other countries which are known or believed to have nuclear weapons or nuclear-weapon technology. These are Britain, France and China, with publicly acknowledged nuclear weapon programs, and India, Israel and South Africa, without acknowledged programs.

## Timing

There is a unique opportunity to freeze US and Soviet nuclear arms in the early 1980s. The planned new US and Soviet ICBMs and the US Pershing II and ground-launched cruise missile are not scheduled to enter production until 1982 or later. The Soviets have offered to negotiate the further deployment of their medium-range nuclear forces and submarine-based forces. Given the pressure to respond to new weapons on both sides and the existing nuclear parity, an equally opportune time for a freeze may not recur for many years.

## Popular Appeal

Campaigns to stop individual weapon systems are some-times treated as unilateral disarmament or circumvented by the development of alternative systems. The pros and cons of the SALT II Treaty are too technical for the patience of the average person. In constrast, an effort to stop the development and production of all US and Soviet nuclear weapons is simple, straightforward, effective and mutual; and for all these reasons it is likely to have great popular appeal. This is essential for creating the scale of popular support that is needed to make nuclear arms control efforts successful.

## Economic Benefits

Although nuclear forces take only a small part of US and Soviet military spending, they do cost some tens of billions of dollars annually. About half of these funds go to existing nuclear forces, while half are budgeted for the testing, production and deployment of new warheads and delivery systems. A nuclear-weapon freeze, accompanied by government-aided conversion of nuclear industries to civilian production, would yield several important economic benefits:

— About $100 billion each (at 1981 prices) would be saved by the United States and the Soviet Union over the period from

1981 to 1990 in unnecessary military spending.

— The savings could be applied to balance the budget; reduce taxes; improve services now being cut back; subsidize home and commercial conversion to safe, renewable energy resources; or increase economic aid to poverty-stricken third world regions, thereby defusing some of the tinderboxes of international conflict.

— With the shift of personnel to more labor-intensive civilian jobs, employment would rise. At the same time, the highly inflationary pressure of military spending would be mitigated.

## Verification

The comprehensive nature of a total freeze on nuclear weapon testing, production and deployment (and, by implication, development) would facilitate verification.

*"I see signs of unreality and dangerous hysteria and fear among some of the advocates of a freeze, and that road can only lead to war."*

# The Case Against a Nuclear Freeze

Robert Michel

Robert Michel is a Republican congressman from the 18th Congressional District of Illinois. The House Republican Leader, he is one of the foremost opponents of nuclear freeze proposals in the country. In the following viewpoint, taken from a speech the congressman delivered on the floor of the House of Representatives (March 30, 1982) during a debate on the Kennedy/Hatfield Congressional Nuclear Freeze Resolution, he outlines his reasons for opposing a nuclear freeze.

Consider the following questions while reading:

1. What five major principles does Congressman Michel claim should be at the heart of any proposal for a nuclear arms freeze?
2. Why does the congressman think the U.S. possession of nuclear weapons prevents war?
3. What advice of Winston Churchill's does he think Americans should heed?

From a speech by Congressman Robert Michel delivered on the floor of the U.S. House of Representatives on March 30, 1982.

Allow me, then, to list what I feel are the five major principles that should be at the heart of any proposal for nuclear arms freeze.

*First,* it must be clearly understood the major issue confronting the world today is not the possession of nuclear arms by the United States, but the defense and preservation of freedom. If freedom cannot be defended through any other means but the possession of a nuclear deterrent by the United States, the possession of such a deterrent is a political and moral imperative on our part.

The current debate, as I see it, is between those who think freedom can be protected without a credible nuclear deterrent on our part, and those who believe — and I am one among them — that such a deterrent is necessary unless and until the Soviet Union poses no nuclear threat.

Any freeze proposal that would place the United States in a position in which our deterrent capability would not be credible is in itself a direct threat to peace.

*Second,* any nuclear freeze must be truly verifiable. Mere adherence to pro forma "verification" is not enough. The verification procedure has to be one that can actually do the job of verifying a freeze on arms reduction.

*Third,* any freeze that would, as a part of its inherent structure, deny us the right to build a B-1 or the MX or the Trident is not acceptable. The Hatfield-Kennedy freeze proposals clearly fall into this category.

*Fourth,* any freeze that does not either directly or indirectly confront the problems of the imbalance of conventional forces now in favor of the Soviet Union is worthless.

*Fifth,* any freeze proposal based on the false idea that the United States is currently engaged in something termed an "arms race" is worthless, because it is not dealing with reality.

The Soviet Union has for 10 years or more been outbuilding, outspending us in the strategic nuclear field. What kind of "race" is it, I ask, when one contestant stops or even moves backward while the other races ahead at full speed? I do not call that a race. I call that a rout.

## U.S. Weapons Prevent War

American possession of nuclear weapons, far from being the scourge of mankind, has for a generation been the only thing that has stood between us and those bent on world domination.

Yes, I would like to see the potential of nuclear war reduced. I think that equal reductions and proper verification over a period of time could at least address one danger we face. But to say that our possession of nuclear arms is in itself a threat is uninformed and dangerous.

If we were to eliminate every nuclear weapon on the face of the Earth tomorrow morning, Soviet tanks could easily overrun

Europe within a couple of days. Let us face it, as it is something we cannot ignore.

Possession of nuclear weapons by the United States at this moment in history is the only means of preventing nuclear war. This means that if we are going to proceed with nuclear arms reduction, such reductions have to be very, very carefully considered. The kind of freeze I favor would have to require strict equality and irrefutable verification procedures.

Courtesy of Field Newspaper Syndicate.

### Freeze Can Lead to War

A nuclear freeze proposal for the sake of a freeze is not acceptable. We are not engaging in some social fad or ideological fashion. We are dealing with the future of freedom.

A nuclear freeze proposal based on hysteria, cowardice, fear, pacifist dogma, misguided enthusiasm, or geopolitical ignorance is unacceptable.

Not all of those who cry, "peace, peace, peace," know how to bring it about. I see signs of unreality and dangerous hysteria and fear among some of the advocates of a freeze, and that road can only lead to war.

Making certain that the Soviet Union realizes we have a credible nuclear and conventional deterrent to its warmaking power is the only way to avoid war. Any freeze proposal that keeps that principle in mind is one I can accept and one the American people, in my judgment, will also accept.

### Conclusion

Let me conclude with the words of a man whose love of

freedom and peace cannot be doubted. This is what he said about the need for a deterrent:

> I have always held the view that the maintenance of peace depends upon the accumulations of deterrents against the aggressor, coupled with a sincere effort to redress grievances.

So said Winston Churchill in the House of Commons on October 5, 1938. Unfortunately, those remarks and comments were not heeded by his countrymen at the time. Will those in the United States who are caught up in the same hysteria that blinded England during the thirties force us to make the same dreadful mistake?

Those who will not learn from history are condemned to relive it...

Lest there be any mistake about it, I think we ought to let the American people know there are many sides to this equation before we can find the right solution.

*"The President's strategic modernization program and the Congress' support for the modernization program will make, or break our attempt to negotiate a reasonable arms control agreement."*

# An American Proposal for Arms Reduction

Alexander M. Haig, Jr.

The former Chief of White House Staff for President Nixon and Supreme Allied Commander Europe, Alexander Haig served as Secretary of State in the Reagan Administration until his resignation on June 25, 1982. On May 11, 1982, Secretary Haig appeared before the Senate Foreign Relations Committee and articulated the U.S. government's position on nuclear arms reductions. Two days earlier, President Reagan, in Eureka, Kansas, had outlined a framework for arms reductions with the Soviets. The following viewpoint, taken from Secretary Haig's testimony, elaborates on the President's requirements for arms reductions.

Consider the following questions while reading:

1. What eight criteria does Secretary Haig claim should be used in judging alternative approaches to strategic arms control?
2. What does the Secretary believe should be our "primary focus" in negotiations?
3. Why does Secretary Haig believe the President's strategic modernization program is vital?
4. Why does Secretary Haig think a nuclear freeze would lessen Soviet incentive for arms reductions?

From testimony given by Alexander M. Haig. Jr.. before the Senate Foreign Relations Committee on June 25, 1982.

The decision to begin negotiations on strategic arms reductions is a crucial element in the President's comprehensive policy framework for arms control. In November we launched America into an entirely new area of arms control, that involving intermediate range nuclear forces. More recently we have begun to participate in efforts within the 40-member Committee on Disarmament to elaborate a total ban on chemical weapons. We are also engaged in discussions in that forum on nuclear testing. In Vienna, negotiations on reductions in conventional forces in Europe are underway. In the coming months, we will renew our efforts to make progress there.

Each of these negotiations is important in its own right. Together, they present an opportunity to strengthen deterrence and to reduce the risk of war at all levels. But it is important to remember that arms control is a means to an end, not an end in itself.

## Our Objective

Our objective is to sustain our national security in a changing international environment and in the face of an expanding Soviet force. Arms control can play a very important part in strengthening our security and restraining the growth of Soviet power through mutually beneficial agreements. But arms control can succeed in this task only if it is coordinated in a strategy that employs the other diplomatic, political, and economic assets at our disposal. This means, among other things, that we must demonstrate our will and capacity to maintain the military balance. It means that we should consult closely with our allies. And it also means that we should seek balanced, equal and verifiable agreements that reduce the risk of war by reinforcing deterrence.

Our preparations for START have reflected these considerations. The President's proposals have also benefitted from the lessons of a decade of American experience with the SALT process. Ironically, the strategic arms competition so troubling to us all reached new heights during the very period when the SALT negotiations seemed so promising.

## Eight Criteria

We therefore developed eight criteria with which to judge alternative approaches to strategic arms control and these have guided our recent decisions on START.

*First*, a START agreement must permit the U.S. to develop and possess sufficient military capability to deter the Soviet Union and to execute the U.S. national military strategy, taking into account the military capability that would be allowed the Soviet Union under such an agreement.

*Second,* an agreement must be based on the principle of

equality. Nothing less than equality is acceptable in the provisions of any future strategic arms limitation agreement for military and political reasons.

*Third*, a START agreement must promote strategic stability by reducing the vulnerability of U.S. strategic forces.

*Fourth,* there must be effective verification with the necessary counting rules, collateral constraints and cooperative measures.

*Fifth,* an agreement must lead to substantial reductions. We took as a given that whatever unit of account was adopted should lend itself to substantial reductions below current levels of forces and that reductions should be to equal ceilings.

*Sixth,* we must be able to explain our objectives and proposals in clear and simple terms to ensure that our START approach would enjoy broad public support.

*Seventh,* our approach had to take into account those matters of particular concern to our allies, including the ability of the U.S. to maintain a credible deterrent, the relationship of the START approach to the INF negotiations and the likelihood of success.

*Eighth* and finally, we needed to devise a sustainable position, which could provide a framework for detailed negotiations, and the basis for an eventual agreement, even in the face of initial Soviet resistance. This meant the position needed to be demonstrably fair, mutually beneficial, and realistic.

## Our Primary Focus

Based upon these criteria, the President has set a new, more demanding goal for strategic arms negotiations. Our objective is to achieve significant reductions in the most destabilizing nuclear systems, especially intercontinental ballistic missiles, thereby strengthening deterrence and stability both for ourselves and for our allies and friends.

To achieve this objective, we will propose to the Soviets in Geneva a practical plan for phased reductions of strategic weapons. This plan is designed to reduce the risk of war by securing agreed steps which will enhance the stability of the strategic balance. Such a goal can be achieved best by negotiating significant reductions in the most destabilizing weapons possessed by both sides — their numbers, their warheads, their overall destructive potential. This will be the primary focus of U.S. efforts.

In Geneva the U.S. will propose that, at the end of the first stage of START reductions, ballistic missile warheads be reduced to equal levels at least one-third below current numbers. The U.S. will propose that, to further enhance stability, no more than half these warheads be deployed on land-based missiles. We wish to see these warhead reductions, as well as significant reductions in deployed missiles, be achieved as quickly as possible.

The conclusion of such an agreement would provide the best possible basis for negotiations leading to a second phase agreement imposing equal ceilings on other elements of U.S and Soviet strategic nuclear forces, including equal limits on ballistic missile throw-weight at less than current U.S. levels. In both phases we will naturally insist on verification procedures to ensure compliance with the agreement.

As President Reagan has noted, these proposals represent a very serious and ambitious undertaking. The sheer physical task of reducing U.S. and Soviet strategic forces and reshaping them to enhance stability will undoubtedly take years of concentrated effort. We believe, however, that the U.S. and the Soviet Union together can remove the instabilities that now exist and reduce significantly nuclear forces on both sides.

## U.S. is Disarmament Leader

Since the end of World War II, the United States has been the leader in serious disarmament and arms control proposals. In 1946, in what became known as the Baruch Plan, the United States submitted a proposal for control of nuclear weapons and nuclear energy by an international authority. The Soviets rejected this plan.

In 1955, President Eisenhower made his open skies proposal, under which the United States and the Soviet Union would have exchanged blueprints of military establishments and provided for aerial reconaissance. The Soviets rejected this plan.

In 1963, the limited test ban treaty came into force. This treaty ended nuclear weapons testing in the atmosphere, outer space or under water by participating nations.

In 1970 the treaty on the nonproliferation of nuclear weapons took effect. The United States played a major role in this key effort to prevent the spread of nuclear explosives and to provide for international safeguards on civil nuclear activities.

My country remains deeply committed to those objectives today and to strengthening the nonproliferation framework. This is essential to international security...

Over the past seven months the United States has put forward a broad-based, comprehensive series of proposals to reduce the risk of war. We have proposed four major points as an agenda for peace:

— Elimination of land-based intermediate-range missiles.

— A one-third reduction in strategic ballistic missile warheads.

— A substantial reduction in NATO and Warsaw Pact ground and air forces.

— And new safeguards to reduce the risk of accidental war.

We urge the Soviet Union today to join with us in this quest.

Ronald Reagan, before the United Nations Second Special Session on Disarmament. June 17, 1982.

## Our Strategic Modernization Program

Our ability to achieve these ambitious goals depends, in large measure, on the Soviets' willingness to negotiate seriously and in good faith. How seriously they will negotiate depends, in turn, on their view of how the military and political environment will look without an agreement. If we fail to adopt the President's military modernization program we will reduce not the nuclear danger, but instead the chances of reaching an arms control agreement on strategic forces. A demonstrated willingness to maintain the balance, through unilateral efforts, if necessary, is as indispensable to the success of our efforts at strategic arms reductions as INF modernization is to the success of the ongoing talks in Geneva. More than any other single defense or political initiative, the President's strategic modernization program and the Congress' support for the modernization program will make, or break, our attempt to negotiate a reasonable arms control agreement.

## A Freeze Would Lessen Soviet Incentive

The need to maintain the Soviet incentive to negotiate reductions in destabilizing options would also be undercut by endorsement of many of the nuclear freeze proposals before us. Most proposals would freeze the existing instabilities and perpetuate existing Soviet advantages. They would eliminate the incentives for the Soviets to negotiate toward the even lower levels of nuclear weapons that we can achieve. We want to go beyond a freeze and do better. We believe we can achieve real reductions and thus lessen the risk of war.

We all understand, and share, the anxiety that motivates those who support the freeze. We all agree that we must not miss this opportunity to make a major step toward meaningful arms control and significant reductions. We are concerned, however, that a freeze on nuclear weapons could frustrate our attempts to achieve stability and balance in this critical area.

The discussions and debates on nuclear policy in the Congress and the country reflect both public concern and our capacity as a democracy to discuss the great issues of today. They have helped to focus American attention on the difficult task ahead of us. We particularly support the objectives set by Senators Warner, Jackson and others for significant reductions in the number of weapons. We hope, however, that this debate will not culminate in fresh battle lines between divided factions, but rather a new national consensus in support of the President's proposal for a fair, realistic and truly beneficial strategic arms agreement.

We feel confident that a better understanding of the needs of deterrence, the state of the military balance and the possibilities for arms control will result in strong support for the initiatives we have taken to modernize our forces, and to reduce the burden of arms, and the risk of war through negotiation. Such support will be crucial in convincing the Soviets that we are determined to compete and at the same time that we are eager to reach a meaningful agreement. The incentives for real arms control exist. We have both the means and the duty to supply them. As we embark on this vital enterprise, now is the time to rally behind the President's proposals.

*"We have always been in favor of substantial reductions of strategic arms."*

# A Soviet Proposal for Arms Reductions

Leonid Brezhnev

Leonid Brezhnev is the General Secretary of the Central Committee of the Communist Party of the Soviet Union and President of the Presidium of the Supreme Soviet of the U.S.S.R. On May 18, 1982, a few days after President Reagan's Eureka, Kansas speech and Secretary Haig's remarks in the previous viewpoint, President Brezhnev presented a Soviet response at the 19th Congress of the Soviet Komsomol (Young Communist League) meeting in the Kremlin. The following viewpoint, taken from President Brezhnev's speech, criticizes the American proposals and offers a Soviet perspective on arms reductions.

Consider the following questions while reading:
1. What step does President Brezhnev claim the Soviets recently took in the European part of the USSR to facilitate arms reductions?
2. Why does President Brezhnev claim that President Reagan's approach to arms reductions talks is unrealistic?
3. What step does President Brezhnev propose be taken at the beginning of arms reductions talks?

From a speech by Leonid Brezhnev, delivered in Moscow to the 19th Congress of the Soviet Komsomol on May 18, 1982.

A session of the United Nations General Assembly is opening in New York within three weeks, a special session entirely devoted to disarmament problems. The Soviet Union, for its part, will do its utmost for the success of the session.

It is now not enough to speak about peace. Specific and practical matters are needed. The key task today in this respect is to de-escalate the nuclear confrontation in Europe, which has reached dangerous levels, to end the further stockpiling of nuclear potential here. It must not be tolerated that a real threat of the outbreak of a world nuclear holocaust be created at any moment in Europe where world wars have begun twice before.

Another round of the talks on the limitation of nuclear arms in Europe will be opened between the USSR and the United States in Geneva within the next few days. Let us watch how the Americans will conduct themselves — will they mark time once again, preparing for the deployment of missiles, or will they show a desire to reach agreement.

### We Have Made Concrete Proposals

The Soviet proposals on this problem are well known. We have come out in favor of the full liquidation of all medium-range nuclear systems in Europe; the West objected that this would go much too far. We proposed that such systems be reduced by more than two-thirds; we are told that this is too little. Well, let us search for mutually acceptable figures. We are also prepared for bigger reductions, of course, on a mutual basis.

To facilitate matters the Soviet Union unilaterally discontinued recently a further deployment of medium-range missiles in the European part of the USSR and decided to reduce a certain number of them. I can report that we are already effecting the reduction of a considerable number of such missiles.

These concrete peaceful actions of our country are regarded approvingly in the world. Some people in the West, however, try to question their importance.

It is being asserted, for example, that the decision adopted by the Soviet Union will not prevent us from continuing to deploy our missiles so as to secure that they, let it be from beyond the Urals, could 'reach' West European countries. I can say in all sureness: No additional medium-range missiles will be deployed in places from which both the FRG and other countries of Western Europe could be within their reach.

A question is also being asked whether the decision adopted by us also envisages a unilateral freeze or the termination of preparations for the deployment of missiles. Yes, it does envisage this, including an end to the construction of launching positions for such missiles.

## Missiles in the Eastern USSR

One more remark. The government of the USA presses for securing that the USSR freeze, and eliminate altogether, the missiles deployed in the eastern part of our country. This is truly an absurd claim! It is possible to handle questions of missiles — their limitation and reduction, but only through negotiations with those in whose hands are the nuclear means which are opposed by our missiles and again, of course, on the basis of reciprocity. We do not object to such negotiations, but, understandably, this is a separate question.

---

## *We Disavow First Use*

Concern for peace is the dominant feature of the Soviet Union's policy. We are convinced that no contradictions between states or groups of states, no differences in social systems, ways of life or ideologies and no transient interests can eclipse the fundamental need of all peoples — the need to safeguard peace and avert a nuclear war.

Today, as never before, purposeful, considered action is required of all states in order to achieve this lofty goal.

Guided by the desire to do all in its power to deliver the peoples from the threat of nuclear devastation and ultimately to exclude its very possibility from the life of mankind, the Soviet state solemnly declares:

The Union of Soviet Socialist Republics assumes the obligation not to be the first to use nuclear weapons.

Leonid Brezhnev, before the United Nations Second Special Session on Disarmament, June 1982.

---

The destinies of war and peace in many respects depend on whether or not a Soviet-U.S. accord is reached on limiting and reducing strategic arms, an honest and fair accord, with no detriment to anyone's interests.

As for the Soviet Union, it has invariably come out in favor of the beginning of talks with the object of working out such an understanding without delay and without any strings attached. This is our position which has been, both in public and through diplomatic channels, made known to the American side.

### Washington's Unrealistic Position

President Reagan, on his part, has now declared that the United States is ready for the resumption of the talks. In our opinion, this is a step in the right direction. It is, however, important that the talks should begin immediately in the right key.

In the same speech the President said that the United States would be in favor of substantial reductions at the talks. Well, we have always been in favor of substantial reductions of strategic arms; there is no need to persuade us in this respect.

But if one looks at the essence of the ideas voiced by the United States President on such reductions, one notes, unfortunately, that the American position is absolutely unilateral in nature. Above all, because the United States would like, in general, to exclude from the talks the strategic arms it is now most intensively developing.

It is not without reason that competent people inside the United States immediately stated that this was an unrealistic position, cut off from life and perhaps simply an insincere position. It is directly prejudicing the security of the USSR and, at the same time, leaves Washington a free hand in the implementation of the American program of stockpiling strategic arms.

One can hardly avoid drawing the conclusion that the position stated by the U.S. President is oriented not to searching for an agreement, but to providing conditions for the continuation of Washington's attempts to achieve military superiority over the Soviet Union.

What is needed for the talks to proceed successfully and to bring about an agreement?

To put it briefly, this requires, first, that the talks should actually pursue the aim of limiting and reducing strategic armaments rather than being a cover for the continued arms race and the breakdown of the existing parity.

Second, it is necessary that both sides should conduct them with due regard for each other's legitimate security interests and strictly in accordance with the principle of equality and equal security.

Last, it is necessary to preserve everything positive that has been achieved earlier. The talks do not start from scratch, but a good deal of far from useless work has been done. This should not be overlooked.

We are convinced that only with this approach can there be any hope for reaching agreement on concrete measures to substantially reduce the strategic armaments of both sides.

It is likewise very important to effectively block all the channels for the continuation of the strategic arms race in any form. This means that the development of new types of strategic weapons should be either banned or restricted to the utmost by agreed upon characteristics.

## Our Proposal

We also have the following proposal.

We would be prepared to reach agreement that the strategic armaments of the USSR and the U.S. be frozen now, as soon as the talks begin — frozen quantitatively — and that their modernization be limited to the utmost.

This cartoon appeared in the June 6-13 edition of *Moscow News*. It accuses the U.S. of using the dove of peace to camouflage nuclear bombs in Europe.

It is also necessary that neither the USA nor the Soviet Union take such actions which would lead to an upsetting of the strategic situation. Such a freeze, an important thing by itself, would facilitate both headway and a radical limitation and reduction of strategic arms.

Briefly, such is our position on the question of strategic weapons.

*"There is no prospect of a solution...We're in a tragic dilemma."*

# The Arms Race Cannot Be Stopped

Joseph Fletcher

Joseph Fletcher is Visiting Professor of Biomedical Ethics at the University of Virginia and a senior editor of *The Churchman* magazine from which this viewpoint is taken. Formerly Professor of Ethics at Episcopal Theological School in Cambridge, Massachusetts, he is the author of a number of books, including *Situation Ethics* (1966), published during the "new morality" controversy that his book helped fuel. In this provocative viewpoint, Dr. Fletcher expresses his hopelessness on the issue of stopping the arms race and implies that civilization is doomed.

Consider the following questions while reading:

1. Why has the author given up hope for stopping the arms race?
2. Why does he see no reasonable hope of even a moral solution?
3. What is the tragic dilemma we find ourselves in?
4. Do you agree with Dr. Fletcher's conclusion?

Joseph Fletcher, "Nuclear War: Can It Be Stopped?" *The Churchman*, February 1982, pp. 14-15. Reprinted with permission.

Let me begin with an epigraph taken from a joint study of nuclear war by former presidents of MIT and the University of California.

> Both sides in the arms race are...confronted by the dilemma of steadily increasing military power and steadily decreasing nation security. *It is our considered judgment that this dilemma has no technical solution.*

*The operative word is "stop," not — as politicians like to suppose — "prevent."*

## No Solution

I've been in about 100 panels at medical centers since 1970. Always before I've tried to bring out the ethical or moral questions involved — in a wide spectrum of problems. I've always suggested a solution or choice of solutions.

But, on this one I'm stumped. I don't think I have a solution, and I don't think anyone else has a solution. Moreover, I don't think there is any solution.

I can deal somehow with suicide — homicide — infanticide — even genocide. These are limited or finite problems. But our problem today is omnicide — nihilism, the ultimate ratio or "final" problem.

Some problems of finite or rational risk and benefit have no technical solution, only a moral solution. Inflation in a free market economy is an example. Population control is another. But in the case of nuclear war I see no reasonable hope of even a moral solution.

Mind you, I am no pacifist. I still stick to the classical conditions of a Just War. But that's a question of conventional weapons, not nuclear. Nuclear war transcends ethics — it's a transmoral problem. It's not like racism or religious bigotry or farm price supports or problems in biomedical ethics. These things are tractable; the arms race is not.

This is a transmoral question because what is the point of thinking about obligation of any kind — personal, mutual or social — if *Homo sapiens* is gone, or even if civilization is gone? Without an ethos there can be no ethics. John Locke's "state of nature" morality won't do so well the second time around.

Military experts have to prepare for the Worst Case, as they say. Nuclear physics has made the worst case annihilation of civilization if not of its builders. (After all, lots of species have been wiped out from trilobites to dinosaurs, although never before by mass suicide.) Tactical nuclear weapons pinpoint their lethal effects, such as the neutron bomb, but strategic weapons (megaton thermonuclear missiles) are lethal for wide areas — and we're stockpiling them! Just one of them can vaporize, incinerate or radiate 12 miles square — cities like Bos-

ton and Washington.

Six countries have them. Nine more could (and may) have them. Twelve more could in six years' time. Four more (including Egypt and Libya) could in seven to ten years.

## No Control

There is no real control of the nuclear race. Polarized between the U.S. and USSR, we've learned that much. In my judgment, however, our jeopardy is not so much from the superpowers as from nuclear proliferation among the "liberationists" of the underdeveloped countries and their terrorist tacticians.

Nobody can win a nuclear war. Nevertheless, Casper Weinberger, Secretary of Defense, says, "...we must make our weapons as indiscriminately destructive as possible, so that we would be deterred from using them." That's a clear statement of the Balance of Terror concept. MAD is the acronym of "mutually assured destruction" — so-called "strategic crisis stability." H. G. Wells called this "Mind at the End of Its Tether" — the title of his last despairing book. It means being rational about our irrational war preparations.

Lewis Thomas in *Medicine and the Bomb* explains why medicine cannot function, cannot help people, would be unable to make even a marginal difference in the human carnage of a nuclear war. Then his mind reaches the end of its tether, because he ends up saying, "We need in a hurry some professionals who can tell us what has gone wrong in the minds of this generation."

There are no pundits to tell us what's wrong, and certainly none to cure it! "Experts" are part of the problem. The International Physicians for Prevention of Nuclear War are at least intellectually honest. Nothing more, though. They can't stop it.

## Our Dilemma

Nobody can. There is no prospect of a solution — ethically, politically or militarily. Fear, mistrust, doubt, defensiveness, are too strong. We're in a tragic dilemma: it would be socially suicidal not to build nuclear weapons, and yet to use them is possibly omnicidal, probably genocidal, at least fatal to civilization. No country is or will be willing to disarm unilaterally. And even if one did, others would not.

---

### Not Much Reason for Optimism

Is a nuclear holocaust inevitable if the arms race is not stopped? Frankly, the answer is almost certainly yes. Now I know that some people feel human beings are so terrified of a nuclear war that no one would dare start one. I wish I could accept that. But neither history nor the Bible gives much reason for optimism.

Billy Graham, *Sojourners*, August 1979.

---

A Princeton undergraduate a few years ago figured out all by himself how to make an atom bomb.

Francis Crick, Nobel laureate and co-discoverer of the structure of DNA, proposes that we seed the rest of the universe with microorganisms by launching them out from the Earth in space capsules — hoping that they will evolve somewhere into higher forms of life. How's that for mind at the end of its tether?

Problems without solutions have a built-in anodyne. It's called "repression." We think about something else. I will. So will you. Letting such things slide back under the mental rug is a blessing, not a curse. We do it quite successfully. Even those who say they think it will be solved "somehow" are sweeping under the rug.

## Is This the End?

Naturally, I hope I'm wrong about this. If we distinguish hope from expectation, as I believe we should, we might hope that what I expect to happen, won't — for unforeseeable reasons. But if my "educated guess" is the right one, those who believe in immortality might feel they have a comforting insurance policy. The rest of us are in parlous shape. We've lost posterity.

The ethical question now is whether war with "nukes" can ever be waged morally, no matter how just the cause. Those who say it can are making the ultimate value choice. They are saying that it is better for those on both sides to be dead than defeated. Is it?

Here is the heart of the matter for us all.

"If ever the time was ripe, it is now...The
dynamics are all on the side of peacemaking."

# The Arms Race
# Can Be Stopped

Herbert Meredith Orrell

Herbert Meredith Orrell is a lecturer of English in the Division
of Continuing Education at the University of New Mexico. A
free lance writer who has written for the *Los Angeles Times*, he
recently wrote an article for *Century* magazine favoring unilateral disarmament titled "Cold Turkey Disarmament". Mr.
Orrell responds to Dr. Fletcher's pessimistic appraisal expressed in the previous viewpoint, by claiming that Dr.
Fletcher's view runs counter to "forces that are evident". The
following viewpoint, taken from *The Churchman* magazine,
which earlier published Dr. Fletcher's view, suggests that the
arms race can be halted.

Consider the following questions while reading:

1. What four reasons does the author present to counter the
   previous viewpoint's claim that the arms race cannot be
   stopped?
2. Why does the author think unilateral disarmament may
   work?
3. What course of action does the author recommend?

Herbert Meredith Orrell, "Dr. Fletcher's Despair," *The Churchman*, April-May, 1982, p. 12. Reprinted with
permission.

I am shocked and dismayed that a man of Dr. Joseph Fletcher's standing as writer, teacher, and theologian, should have declared flatly that he sees no solution for halting the nuclear arms race. I believe that Dr. Fletcher's argument runs counter to forces which are clearly evident. Let me cite some of them.

*First,* the anti-nuclear movement in Europe represents a tremendous outpouring of moral indignation at the outrage of nuclear war. So loud is the outcry, indeed, that Helmut Schmidt of West Germany has been forced to oppose the deployment of Pershing missiles on European soil. Other NATO countries have taken similar stands. President Reagan himself, in order to neutralize the peace movement, has been compelled to initiate arms talks with the Russians, even in the face of strong opposition from rightists.

*Second,* new groups are springing up almost daily in the U.S. to oppose the squandering of money and resources on nuclear weaponry. Churches hitherto silent are now calling for a freeze on nuclear weapons. The United Presbyterian Church in America has urged all members to be active peacemakers.

*Third,* polls generally show that Americans want peace with the Russians, even though they are skeptical that agreements will be honored.

*Fourth,* Americans are becoming increasingly aware that the enormous sums spent on weapons are hurting the poor and gutting sorely needed social programs. Arms expenditures also produce inflation because dollars spent on nonproductive goods inexorably cause price increases in consumer goods. Nor do arms expenditures relieve unemployment, because jobs in defense nearly always require technical skills that most of those out of work do not have.

### Unilateral Disarmament

I also take exception to Dr. Fletcher's assertion that we cannot undertake unilateral disarmament because no other country would follow suit. But, considering the Russian disarmament proposals over the years — proposals which the United States has consistently rejected without so much as considering them — the Russians would be only too ready and happy to reciprocate any move by the United States with disarmament of their own.

Whatever else the Russians may be, they are not stupid. They know they are encircled and outnumbered in the instruments of war. They want peace. They know there can be only losers in a nuclear war. Their economy is foundering and they need to spend all their energy in salvaging it. If we would only let up on our unremitting pressure on the Soviets — threats, provocations, warlike gestures, and now, the latest, economic sanctions — I am confident they would be willing to approach the bargaining table in good faith.

As for the access by terrorists to nuclear weapons, this will continue to be a danger until we make honest efforts to cope with the causes of terrorism rather than spend our money and energy in fruitless efforts to wipe it out.

### The Time Is Ripe

What needs to be done now, I believe, is to organize the various peace movements into a solid phalanx of protest and opposition to the Reagan war policies. I call again, as I have in the past, for a coalition of artists, academics, labor leaders, philosophers who will come out strongly for unilateral initiatives for peace. Such a coalition could instigate and support nation-wide strikes and demonstrations to jam the gears of the war machine if Reagan or Congress refuse to take action.

If ever the time was ripe, it is now. What theologians call the *kairos* —the intersection of potentials with human hopes and expectations — is now present. The dynamics are all on the side of peacemaking.

Let us not miss out on what might be the final opportunity to reverse the course of the arms race. Let us not succumb to the death wish. Rather, let us keep in mind that mankind has too much to be proud of to let it be destroyed by monstrous, indecent weapons. Let every man and woman withhold support from an American imperium gone mad and corrupt, just as the early Christians refused to back a decaying and ruthless Roman empire.

Let not the mentally and physically sick drag down our lovely world into the pit of destruction.

# Distinguishing Bias From Reason

Because it involves issues like patriotism and human survival, the subject of the arms race often generates great emotional responses in people. When dealing with such a highly controversial subject, many will allow their feelings to dominate their powers of reason. Thus, one of the most important basic thinking skills is the ability to distinguish between opinions based upon emotion or bias and conclusions based upon a rational consideration of the facts.

The following statements are taken from the viewpoints in the last chapter of this book. Consider each statement carefully. *Mark R for any statement you believe is based on reason or a rational consideration of the facts. Mark B for any statement you believe is based on bias, prejudice or emotion. Mark I for any statement you think is impossible to judge.*

If you are doing this activity as the member of a class or group, compare your answers with those of other class or group members. Be able to defend your answers. You may discover that others will come to different conclusions than you. Listening to the rationale others present for their answers may give you valuable insights in distinguishing between bias and reason.

If you are reading this book alone, ask others if they agree with your answers. You too will find this interaction very valuable.

> *R = a statement based on reason*
> *B = a statement based on bias*
> *I = a statement impossible to judge*

_____ 1. To improve national and international security, the United States and the Soviet Union should stop the nuclear arms race.

_____ 2. A freeze on nuclear missiles and aircraft can be verified by existing national means.

_____ 3. Any freeze that does not either directly or indirectly confront the problems of the imbalance of conventional forces now in favor of the Soviet Union is worthless.

_____ 4. The Russians would be only too ready and happy to reciprocate any move by the United States with disarmament of their own.

_____ 5. American possession of nuclear weapons, far from being the scourge of mankind, has for a generation been the only thing that has stood between us and those bent on world domination.

_____ 6. A freeze would hold constant the existing nuclear parity between the United States and the Soviet Union.

_____ 7. No country is or will be willing to disarm unilaterally.

_____ 8. If we were to eliminate every nuclear weapon on the face of the earth tomorrow morning, Soviet tanks could easily overrun Europe within a couple of days.

_____ 9. It is not enough to speak about peace. Specific and practical matters are needed.

_____ 10. The major issue confronting the world today is not the possession of nuclear arms by the United States, but the defense and preservation of freedom.

_____ 11. Nobody can win a nuclear war.

_____ 12. There is no prospect of a solution — ethically, politically or militarily...We're in a tragic dilemma; it would be socially suicidal not to build nuclear weapons, and yet to use them is possibly omnicidal.

_____ 13. A nuclear-weapon freeze, accompanied by government-aided conversion of nuclear industries would save at least $100 billion each in U.S. and Soviet military spending (at today's prices) in 1981-1990.

# Bibliography

The following list of periodical articles deals with the subject matter of this chapter.

Robert J. Bresler — "Beyond the Nuclear Freeze," *USA Today*, July 1982, p. 6.

Leonid Brezhnev — "Disarmament: To Bring About An Agreement," *Vital Speeches of the Day*, June 15, 1982, p. 515.

McGeorge Bundy — "No First Use Needs Careful Study," *The Bulletin of the Atomic Scientists*, June/July 1982, p. 6.

Frank Chapple — "Masters of Manipulation," *Reader's Digest*, June 1982, p. 68.

Edward Jay Epstein — "Disinformation: Or, Why the CIA Cannot Verify an Arms-Control Agreement," *Commentary*, July 1982, p. 21.

Gregory A. Fossendal — "Exploring The High Frontier: New Defense Would Stifle Soviets, Help Chances For Peace," *Conservative Digest*, June 1982, p. 3.

Albert Gore, Jr. — "The Fork In The Road," *The New Republic*, May 5, 1982, p. 13.

William E. Griffith — "Perspective On The Peace Movement: Ban *Whose* Bomb?, *Reader's Digest*, June 1982, p. 65.

Mark O. Hatfield vs. Richard R. Burt — "Pro and Con: A Freeze On Nuclear Weapons?" *U.S. News and World Report*, April 5, 1982, p. 55.

Mary Kaldor — "What the Peace Movement Really Means," *The Nation*, June 26, 1982, p. 778.

Karl Kaiser & Others — "Nuclear Weapons and the Preservation of Peace: A German Response," *Foreign Affairs*, Summer 1982, p. 1157.

William Kohlmann — "Our Missing Link," *Newsweek*, July 26, 1982, p. 13.

Sidney Lens — "Ban The Bomb," *The Progressive*, August 1982, p. 24.

"How Deep A Freeze?" *The Progressive*, May 1982, p. 16.

George Marotta — "Peace Movement Serves Soviet Purposes," *Conservative Digest*, June 1982, p. 7.

*Newsweek* — "A Matter Of Life And Death," April 26, 1982, p. 20.

Christopher Paine — "The Freeze And The United Nations," *The Bulletin of the Atomic Scientists*, June/July 1982, p. 10.

Peter Pringle                "Putting World War III On Ice," *Inquiry*, July 1982, p. 13.

*The Progressive*          "Reagan's Nuclear Shell Game," July 1982, p. 9.

Ronald Reagan          "The Atlantic Alliance: Arms Control and Reduction," *Vital Speeches of the Day*, July 1, 1982, p. 550.

"East-West Relations: Reduction of Nuclear Arms," *Vital Speeches of the Day*, June 1, 1982, p. 482.

"Nuclear Arms Race: Free of Fear," *Vital* Speeches of the Day, July 15, 1982, p. 578.

"Our First Obligation Is Freedom: Arms Reduction," *Vital Speeches of the Day*, June 15, 1982, p. 515.

John P. Roche           "Anti-Nuke Capers," *National Review*, March 19, 1982, p. 318.

Eugene V. Rostow      "America's Blueprint for Controlling Nuclear Weapons," *Department of State Bulletin*, August 1981, p. 59.

*Time*                     "For And Against A Freeze," March 29, 1982, p. 16.

John Train              "Naivete Can Kill You," *Forbes*, July 5, 1982, p. 45.

Paul C. Warnke         "Nuclear Arms Control: Its Politics And Prospects," *New Catholic World*, March/April 1982, p. 52.

George F. Will           "A 'Simple' Freeze Means Complex Dangers For U.S.," *Conservative Digest*, 1982, p. 6.

# Appendixes

# I. Organizations to Contact

**American Enterprise Institute for Policy Research**
1150 17th Street N.W.
Washington, DC 20036
(202) 862-5800

The Institute, founded in 1943, is a conservative think tank that researches a number of issues, including foreign policy and defense. A subscription to *Foreign Policy and Defense Review,* published bi-monthly, costs $18 a year.

**Americanism Educational League**
P.O. Box 5986
Buena Park, CA 90622
(714) 828-5040

The League, founded in 1927, campaigns on behalf of private ownership of property, strong national defense, strict crime control and limited government conducted within balanced budgets. It periodically publishes position papers and pamphlets on national defense issues.

**Arms Control and Disarmament Agency**
U.S. Department of State
Washington, DC 20451
(202) 632-3597

This government agency publishes information on disarmament treaties, on-going negotiations and other arms control issues. It occasionally does studies on the military balance and annually publishes *World Military Expenditures and Arms Transfers.*

**Arms Control Association**
11 Dupont Circle N.W.
Washington, DC 20036
(202) 797-6450

This non-partisan association, founded in 1971, does research on practical and theoretical questions of arms control. A subscription to *Arms Control Today,* published eleven times a year, costs $25, $10 for students.

**Center For Defense Information**
Capitol Gallery West
600 Maryland Avenue S.W.
Washington, DC
(202) 484-9490

The Center, founded in 1972, as a non-partisan research organization, provides up-to-date information and analyses of the U.S. military. A subscription to *The Defense Monitor,* published ten times a year, is included in its annual $25 membership fee.

**Center For War/Peace Studies**
218 E. 18th Street
New York, NY 10003
(212) 475-0850

The Center was originally founded in 1966 as a program of the New York Friends Group. It carries out in-depth studies of global problems, including arms control. A subscription to *Global Report*, published four times a year, is included in its annual $20 membership fee. Students may subscribe for $5 a year.

**Christian Anti-Communist Crusade**
P.O. Box 890
227 E. Sixth Street
Long Beach, CA 90801
(213) 437-0941

The Crusade, founded in 1953, sponsors anti-subversive seminars "to inform Americans of the philosophy, morality, organization, techniques and strategy of Communism and associated forces." Its newsletter, published semi-monthly, is free.

**Coalition For A New Foreign and Military Policy**
120 Maryland Avenue N.E.
Washington, DC 20002
(202) 546-8400

The Coalition, founded in 1976, united 44 national religious, labor, peace, research and social action organizations working for a "peaceful, non-interventionist and demilitarized U.S. foreign policy." It works to reduce military spending, protect human rights and promote arms control and disarmament. A subscription to *Coalition Close-Up*, published quarterly, and other publications, is included in its annual $20 membership fee.

**Committee For Nuclear Responsibility**
Box 11207
San Francisco, CA 94101

The Committee, founded in 1971, proposes ways to eliminate nuclear power and nuclear arms. It publishes occasional papers and flyers on nuclear issues.

**Committee On the Present Danger**
1800 Massachusetts Avenue N.E.
Washington, DC 20036
(202) 466-7444

The Committee, founded in 1976, describes its functions as directing attention to the unfavorable military balance between the United States and the Soviet Union. It publishes occasional papers dealing with this issue.

**Congressional Budget Office**
Office of Intergovernmental Relations
House Annex #2
2nd and D Streets S.W.
Washington, DC 20515

The CBO is an agency of Congress established to review the budgetary implications of various programs. Budget issue papers consider a host of narrow issues, but also very broad strategic analyses. Write for a list of publications. All CBO publications can be received free.

**Council For A Livable World**
100 Maryland Avenue N.E.
Washington, DC 20002
(202) 543-4100

The Council, founded in 1962, is a public interest group which raises funds for Senatorial candidates who work for arms control, and which lobbies on arms control and military budget issues. It publishes study papers and fact sheets on issues of foreign policy and arms control.

**Council For the Defense of Freedom**
P.O. Box 28526
Washington, DC 20005
(202) 783-6736

The Council, founded in 1951, is concerned about "the mortal danger we face if we do not stop communist aggression." Its weekly paper, *The Washington Inquirer*, repeatedly deals with the arms race and "our failure to take measures to overcome our lack of preparedness." A subscription is $20 a year.

**Council On Economic Priorities**
84 Fifth Avenue
New York, NY 10011
(212) 691-8550

The Council, founded in 1969, disseminates information on a number of economic issues, including military contracting and spending. Its newsletter, published eight to twelve times a year, is included in its annual membership fee of $15 a year. Students may join for $7.50 a year. Also included with membership are several studies and reports.

**Department of Defense**
Office of Public Affairs
Public Correspondence Division
Room 2E 777
Washington, DC 20037

Write for a list of publications and an order form.

**Fellowship of Reconciliation**
Box 271
Nyack, NY 10960
(914) 358-4601

FOR, founded in 1915, is a pacifist organization, made up of religious pacifists drawn from all faiths. It "attempts, through education and action, to substitute nonviolence and reconciliation for violence in international relations." It publishes pamphlets, books, cards and the monthly *Fellowship* dealing with disarmament and nonviolence. A subscription to *Fellowship* is $6 a year.

**Foreign Policy Association**
205 Lexington Avenue
New York, NY 10016
(212) 481-8450

The Association, founded in 1918, is a non-partisan educational organization that deals with foreign policy issues. It publishes a wide range of publications dealing with foreign policy.

**The Heritage Foundation**
513 C Street N.E.
Washington, DC 20002
(202) 546-4400

The Foundation, founded in 1974, is "dedicated to limited government, individual and economic freedom and a strong national defense." It publishes research in various formats on national defense. A subscription to *National Security Record*, published monthly, is $25 a year.


**Institute For Defense and Disarmament Studies**
251 Harvard Street
Brookline, MA 92146
(617) 734-4216

The Institute, incorporated in 1980, was founded "to study the nature and purposes of military forces and the obstacles to and opportunities for disarmament." It publishes an annual survey of *World Military Forces & Disarmament Opportunities* and other disarmament materials.


**Institute For Policy Studies**
1901 Q Street N.W.
Washington, DC 20009
(202) 234-9382

The Institute, founded in 1963, is a research and public education center which publishes a variety of books, reports and issues papers on international affairs. Write for a catalog of its publications.


**Pax Christi USA**
6337 W. Cornelia Avenue
Chicago, IL 60634
(312) 736-2114

Founded in 1973, Pax Christi is a Roman Catholic peace movement, dedicated to "building peace and justice by exploring and articulating the ideal of Christian nonviolence." It works for disarmament, a just world order, selective conscientious objection, education for peace and alternatives to violence. It publishes occasional papers and a quarterly newsletter which can be obtained by making a voluntary contribution.


**Physicians For Social Responsibility**
639 Massachusetts Avenue
Cambridge, MA 02139
(617) 491-2754

This organization of medical doctors has more than 100 chapters in cities throughout the country. The group holds periodic symposia to alert people to the medical consequences of nuclear war. Founded in 1979, annual membership is $30 and student membership is $10.


**SANE**
514 C Street N.E.
Washington, DC 20002
(202) 546-7100

SANE was founded in 1957 "to bring about negotiated settlement of international disputes and major cuts in arms spending." Its membership fee of $20 a year, $10 for students, includes action alerts, issue analyses and a subscription to *Sane World* which is published monthly.

**Soviet Embassy**
Information Department
1706 18th Street N.W.
Washington, DC 20009

Speeches and statements on disarmament and Soviet foreign policy are available. It is best to ask for a specific speech or publication.


**U.S. Government Accounting Office**
Document Handling and Information Services Facility
P.O. Box 6015
Gaithersburg, MD 20760

The GAO reviews the general efficiency of government administration and particular procurement programs. It is a good source of authoritative critques of Pentagon programs. Write for the *Monthly List of GAO Reports,* which includes an order form. A single copy of any GAO report is free.


**War Resisters League**
339 Lafayette Street
New York, NY 10012
(212) 0450

WRL, founded in 1923, is a national pacifist organization opposed to armaments, conscription and war. *WRL News*, published every other month, is free. *Win* magazine is $20 a year.

# II. Bibliography

**BOOKS**

| | |
|---|---|
| Ruth Adams & Susan Cullen, eds. | *The Final Epidemic: Physicians and Scientists On Nuclear War.* Chicago: The Educational Foundation For Nuclear Science, 1981. |
| Richard J. Barnet | *Real Security: Restoring American Power In A Dangerous Decade.* New York: Simon and Schuster, 1981. |
| Congressional Quarterly | *U.S. Defense Policy.* Washington, D.C.: Congressional Quarterly, 1980. |
| Joseph D. Douglas & Amoretta M. Hoeber | *Soviet Strategy For Nuclear War.* Stanford, Calif.: Hoover Institution Press, 1971. |
| Theodore Draper | *Defending America.* New York: Basic Books, 1977. |
| Samuel Glasstone & Phillip J. Dolan, eds. | *The Effects of Nuclear Weapons.* Washington, D.C.: Department of Defense, 1977. |
| Peter Goodwin | *Nuclear War: The Facts Of Our Survival.* New York: The Rutledge Press, 1981. |
| Daniel O. Graham | *High Frontier: A New National Strategy.* Washington, D.C.: The Heritage Foundation, 1982. |
| Ground Zero | *Nuclear War: What's In It For You?* New York: Pocket Books, 1982. |
| International Institute For Strategic Studies | *The Military Balance 1981-82.* London: International Institute For Strategic Studies, 1981. |
| Mary Kaldor | *The Baroque Arsenal.* New York: Hill and Wang, 1981. |
| Edward Kennedy & Mark Hatfield | *Freeze! How You Can Help Prevent Nuclear War.* New York: Bantam Books, 1982. |
| Christopher A. Kojm | *The ABC's Of Defense: America's Military In the 1980s.* New York: The Foreign Policy Association, 1981. |
| Sidney Lens | *The Day Before Doomsday: An Anatomy of the Nuclear Arms Race.* New York: Doubleday & Company, 1977. |
| William P. Lineberry | *Arms Control.* New York: H.W. Wilson Company, 1979. |
| Andrew J. Pierre | *The Global Politics Of Arms Sales.* Princeton, N.J.: Princeton University Press, 1982. |
| Jonathan Schell | *The Fate Of the Earth.* New York: Alfred A. Knopf, 1982. |
| Nikolai V. Sivachev & Nikolai N. Yakovlev | *Russia and the United States.* Chicago: University of Chicago Press, 1979. (Describes U.S.-Soviet relations from a Soviet point of view.) |

V.D. Skoloskiy — *Soviet Military Strategy.* New York: Crane, Russak & Company, 1975.

Stockholm International Peace Research Foundation — *Armaments and Disarmament In the Nuclear Age.* Atlantic Highlands, N.J.: Humanities Press, 1976.

W. Scott Thompson, ed. — *From Weakness To Strength: National Security in the 1980s.* San Francisco: Institute for Contemporary Studies, 1980.

GeorgeWeigel — *The Peace Bishops and the Arms Race.* Chicago: World Without War Council, 1982.

Caspar W. Weinberger — *Annual Report To the Congress.* Washington, D.C.: Superintendent of Documents, 1982.


## PAMPHLETS

American Friends Service Committee — *Makers Of the Nuclear Holocaust.* American Friends Service Committee, 1981. Available for $1.25 from AFSC, 1660 Lafayette, Denver, CO 80218.

Marion Anderson — *The Impact Of Military Spending On the Machinists Union.* International Association of Machinists, 1979. Available free from IAM, Room 1007, 1300 Connecticut Ave. N.W., Washington, D.C. 20036.

Jeffrey G. Barlow, ed. — *Reforming the Military.* The Heritage Foundation, 1981. Available for $3.00 from The Heritage Foundation, 513 C St., N.E., Washington, D.C. 20002.

Robert DeGrasse & others — *The Costs and Consequences of Reagan's Military Buildup.* The Council On Economic Priorities, 1982. Available for $2.50 from IAM, same as above.

Department of Defense — *Soviet Military Power.* Department of Defense, 1981. Available for $6.50 from Superintendent of Documents, U.S. Government Printing Office, Washington, D.C. 20402 — Document #008-000-00358-1.

Foreign Policy Association — *SALT II: Toward Security Or Danger?* Foreign Policy Association, 1979. Available for $2.00 from FPA, 345 East 46 St., New York, NY 10017.

Samuel T. Francis — *The Soviet Strategy Of Terror.* The Heritage Foundation, 1981. Available for $2.00 from The Heritage Foundation, same as above.

Colin S. Gray — *Strategy and the MX.* The Heritage Foundation, 1980. Available for $2.00 from the Heritage Foundation, same as above.

Sojourners — *A Matter Of Faith.* Sojourners, 1981. Available for $3.50 from Sojourners, 1309 L St., N.W., Washington, D.C. 20005.

| United Nations | *The Arms Race Or the Human Race?* 1981 and *Disarmament Fact Sheets* which are published sporadically. For current price list describing these two publications and others, contact Center for Disarmament, United Nations, New York, NY 10017. |
| --- | --- |
| Western Goals | *The War Called Peace.* Western Goals, 1982. Available for $5.00 from Western Goals, 309A Cameron St., Alexandria, VA 22314. |
| Young Americans For Freedom | *Zero Option.* Young Americans For Freedom, 1982. Available free from YAF, Box 1002, Woodland Rd., Sterling, VA 22170. |

## MAGAZINES

| *The Bulletin Of the Atomic Scientists* | June 1982. Numerous articles on the nuclear arms race. |
| --- | --- |
| *Christianity and Crisis* | January 18, 1982. Special issue on nuclear arms and disarmament. |
| *Commonweal* | August 13, 1982. Special issue on Catholic bishops and nuclear weapons. |
| *Conservative Digest* | June 1982. Section on the High Frontier and conservative reactions to the peace movement. |
| *Current* | July/August 1982. Section on nuclear weapons and war. |
| *Current History* | October 1981. Entire issue on the Soviet Union. |
| *Defense 82* | A monthly magazine published by the Department of Defense to provide official and professional information to commanders and key personnel on matters related to defense policies. |
| *Department of Defense Bulletin* | May 1982. Section on arms control, including very visual atlas of current military forces. |
| *Engage/Social Action* | April 1982. Special issue on the arms race. |
| *Focus* | March/April 1980. Special issue on the world arms trade. |
| *Foreign Affairs* | Winter 1981/82. Section on nuclear weapons in the 1980s. |
| *The Internationalist* | March 1981. Special issue on the nuclear arms race. |
| *NATO Review* | June 1982. Special edition on peace and security. |
| *New Catholic World* | March/April 1982. Special issue on arms control. |
| *Sojourners* | February 1977. Special issue on nuclear weapons. |
| *The Witness* | June 1982. Special issue on the Christian's response to nuclear weapons. |

# III. Chronology of Arms Race Events

| | |
|---|---|
| August 6, 1945 | U.S. drops the first atomic bomb on Hiroshima. Eighty thousand people are killed instantly and another seventy thousand die within a month. |
| August 9, 1945 | U.S. drops a larger atomic bomb on Nagasaki. |
| September 23, 1949 | President Truman announces that the U.S.S.R. has tested an atomic bomb. |
| October 3, 1952 | Great Britain explodes its first atomic bomb. |
| November 1, 1952 | U.S. explodes first hydrogen bomb. |
| 1958 (date uncertain) | Nuclear wastes plant explodes in Russia's Ural Mountains, killing untold numbers of people, causing widespread radiation sickness and poisoning hundreds of square miles of land. |
| February 13, 1960 | France explodes its first atomic bomb. |
| June 10, 1963 | President Kennedy announces that the U.S., Britain, and the U.S.S.R. have agreed to negotiations seeking a ban on nuclear weapons tests. The ban became effective October 10, 1963. |
| October 16, 1964 | China explodes its first atomic bomb. |
| January 17, 1966 | U.S. atomic bomb is lost in air crash over Spain. |
| October 10, 1967 | Sixty countries, including U.S. and U.S.S.R., agree to ban weapons of mass destruction from outer space. |
| March 11, 1968 | Nuclear Nonproliferation Treaty, prohibiting transfer of nuclear weapons from nuclear weapon countries to non-nuclear weapons countries, is adopted by U.N. and signed by 103 countries. |
| October 3, 1972 | Strategic Arms Limitation Treaty (SALT) freezes the total number of U.S. and U.S.S.R. offensive and defensive missile launchers. |
| May 18, 1974 | India explodes its first nuclear bomb. |
| June 18, 1979 | SALT II Treaty, a comprehensive treaty limiting strategic offensive weapons, is signed by the U.S. but not ratified by the U.S. Senate. |
| February 21, 1980 | CBS reports that Israel detonated an atomic bomb off the coast of Africa with assistance from South Africa on September 22, 1979. |
| August 9, 1981 | President Reagan announces his decision to develop and stockpile neutron bombs, which leave building and armaments intact while destroying human life. |
| August 13, 1981 | The U.S.S.R. announces its plan to develop and stockpile neutron bombs. |

| March 10, 1982 | Senators Edward Kennedy and Mark Hatfield introduce a Senate Resolution calling for the U.S. and the U.S.S.R. to negotiate a freeze on nuclear weapons development. |
| --- | --- |
| March 31, 1982 | Senators Henry Jackson and John Warner introduce a Senate Resolution calling for a freeze after U.S. catches up to Soviets. |
| March 31, 1982 | President Reagan claims "the Soviet Union does have a definite margin of superiority." He supports the Jackson/Warner Resolution. |
| April 18-25, 1982 | "Ground Zero Week" spurs hundreds of thousands of freeze supporters to demonstrate in cities in the U.S. |
| May 9, 1982 | President Reagan proposes a nuclear reduction plan calling for both the U.S. and the U.S.S.R. to cut the number of warheads on land based missiles by one third. |
| May 18, 1982 | Leonid Brezhnev, Russian leader, responds to the Reagan proposal, claiming it would reduce Soviet forces more than American. He counters with a proposal to freeze weapons during arms negotiations talks. |
| June 7, 1982 | United Nations convenes Second Special Session on Disarmament. |
| June 29, 1982 | U.S. and U.S.S.R. begin talks to limit and reduce strategic nuclear arms. |

# IV. Glossary of Terms

**ABM** antiballistic missile; designed to intercept and destroy another ballistic missile

**annihilation** total destruction

**Armageddon** a great and decisive — final — battle

**Auschwitz** notorious death camp in World War II where many thousands of Jews and others were destroyed in massive gas ovens

**ballistic missiles** consist of a powering rocket and a payload (warhead); after the rocket establishes the path and velocity, it shuts off and/or separates from the payload which continues, with the help of gravity, to the target; can be used over extremely long distances

**beatitude** statement of a way to achieve blessedness, especially one of those stated by Jesus in the Sermon on the Mount

**Bolshevism** originally, the political philosophy of the radical marxists who seized the Russian government in 1917; often used as a synonym for communism

**CIA** Central Intelligence Agency; coordinates the intelligence activities of U.S. government departments and agencies in the interest of national security

**containment policy** attempt by U.S. to "contain" Communism, not let it spread, through financial and military aid to countries viewed as vulnerable to its influence, and by the encirclement of military bases and forces.

**Department of Defense** the part of the U.S. government which regulates the military services and is responsible for defending the nation

**deployment** the spreading out or distributing of something, particularly military forces and arms

**detente** a relaxation of international tension between the Cold War adversaries, usually brought about by a treaty or agreement

**deterrence** prevention, restraint; belief that strong military capabilities will deter attack or aggression from another country

**Eastern Europe** those European countries most closely connected — geographically, philosophically, and/or politically — with the Soviet Union

**escalation** a stepping up, increasing, intensifying

**fiscal year** twelve consecutive months, not necessarily starting with January, established by a country, company, or individual as their financial year

**GDP** Gross Domestic Product; similar to GNP (below) but excludes imports and exports

**Geneva** city in Switzerland used as site for many peace talks

**GNP** Gross National Product; total monetary value of all goods and services produced in a country in a year

**hawk** slang term for people who believe in strong military defense and aggressive stance toward other countries

**hegemony** leadership or dominance

**holocaust** devastation, destruction

**ICBMs** Intercontinental Ballistic Missiles; missiles that are capable of traveling great distances from one continent to another

**ideology** system of beliefs or doctrines

**imperialism** extending governmental rule and/or influence over foreign countries

**INF** Intermediate-range Nuclear Forces

**intelligence networks** agencies that gather information, often secret, often acquired by subterfuge, about other governments

**Joint Chiefs of Staff** a chairman and the heads of the Armed Services (Army, Navy, Air Force) who advise the President about defense policy

**Kremlin** the building that houses the executive branch of the Russian government; also used as a synonym for that branch

**MIRV** Multiple Independent Targetable Reentry Vehicle; enables several warheads on a ballistic missile to be directed to separate locations

**MRV** Multiple Reentry Vehicle; a ballistic missile with several warheads which cannot be separately targeted

**NATO** North Atlantic Treaty Organization; a group of countries in Europe and North America which have agreed to support, defend, and aid each other politically and militarily

**Nonproliferation Treaty** first signed in 1968; signing nations without nuclear weapons agreed to continue without them; those nations with nuclear weapons agreed to work to prevent their spread and to aid in the development of peaceful uses of nuclear energy

**"nuke"** slang term for nuclear, often referring to nuclear weapons

**omnicide** killing everything; annihilation

**pacifism** opposed to war and violence

**parity** equality

**Pentagon** building that houses the U.S. Department of Defense; used as a synonym for military policy and policy makers

**preemptive** first; to do something before someone else gets a chance to

**priority targeting** choosing the most vital targets to be destroyed first

**"pro forma"** according to form; in form only, not actual

**proxy forces** military personnel and equipment which purport to belong to the country they are fighting for but which in fact are funded and/or commanded by an outside country for its own purposes of influence and power

**rearmament** to acquire and build up an arsenal after a period of having few arms or weapons, or having slowed down in their production and accumulation

**reciprocity** to be able to give back what is given or its equivalent

**SALT** Strategic Arms Limitations Talks; a series of negotiations between the US and USSR, begun in 1969, attempting to limit the production, acquisition, maintenance, and use of strategic weapons

**SLBMs** Submarine Launched Ballistic Missiles; also **SLCM** Submarine Launched Cruise Missiles

**Soviets** the governing officials or the people of the Soviet Union (see U.S.S.R.)

**START** Strategic and Tactical Arms Reduction Talks; President Reagan's proposal, made in 1981, to further limit the use and production of nuclear weapons

**strategic weapons** generally refers to long-range weapons, often capable of going thousands of miles

**subversion** undermining, corrupting, in a secretive, underhanded way

**surrogate** substitute

**tactical weapons** used on battlefields or limited distance situations

**Third World** developing nations, especially of Asia, Africa, and South America, not aligned with either the NATO nations or the Warsaw Pact nations, considered as a potential political force to be wooed by both groups

**totalitarian** government with strong authoritarian control concentrated in a single political party

**tractable** easily managed or controlled

**TRIAD** combination of ICBMs, SLBMs, and intercontinental bombers, each of which presents different defensive problems to an enemy

**unilateral** done by only one person, group, or nation

**U.S.S.R.** Union of Soviet Socialist Republics; a group of 15 politically connected nations in Eastern Europe and Northern and Western Asia, of which Russia is the largest

**Vienna** capital city of Austria, used as the site of the SALT talks

**warheads** the forward section of a missile containing the explosive; the bomb

**Warsaw Pact** alliance of Russia and the Communist countries in Eastern Europe, established in response to NATO

**watershed** a major turning point

**"the West"** Western Europe and North America

**"window of vulnerability"** term used by President Reagan in 1981 to describe what he believed was the U.S.'s inability to defend itself in the event of a surprise attack

*The Arms Control Association (see address on page 149) distributes a very helpful booklet, **A Glossary of Arms Control Terms**. Single copies are available free.*

# Index

162